Praise

'A rich and insightful guide for leaders navigating today's disruptive world. Rochelle blends lived experience, grounded research, and practical reflection in a way that feels both real and usable. A book for those who want to lead through pressure and change, while still being yourself.'

— **Han-Peter Gai**, Chief Executive Officer

'A grounded, hopeful, and deeply relevant guide for today's leaders. Rochelle brings together research, realism, and compassion to show that thriving within the system is not only possible but powerful. A book to return to whenever the pace feels too fast to breathe.'

— **Rute Fernandes**, Pharmaceuticals Executive

'This work prompted deep introspection about my own journey, the patterns I've carried, and which ones I now choose to change. Through Rochelle's vulnerable sharing, I'm reminded that true leadership begins with continuous self-realignment. It will not only make me a better leader, but also truer to myself and those I'm privileged to impact.'

— **Rozanne Leyds**, Partner, Big Four Professional Services firm

'Humble, truthful, and quietly provoking. Rochelle brings lived experience and sage guidance together in a powerful reflection for anyone striving to lead with purpose and alignment.'

— **April Ho-Nishimura**, Global Customer Experience Executive

'A treasure trove of wisdom for anyone who loves the world of work yet feels its weight. Rochelle invites us to stay in the system, not to escape it, and to rediscover energy, balance, and purpose from within. Her writing honours both the intelligence of organisations and the humanity of the people who keep them alive.'

— **Teresa Mazur**, Global HR Executive

'Brilliant in its depth and clarity – a rare blend of learning, healing, and performance. Rochelle's book is gripping, reflective, and real; a companion to return to, not just read once.'

— **Karen Rivoire**, HR Executive and Board Adviser

'A powerful, deeply practical guide for anyone ready to move from surviving to truly thriving. Rochelle brings clarity, honesty, and heart to a complex topic, helping readers see that while the system may not change overnight, we can.'

— **Marina Cvetkovic**, CEO and Board Adviser

'This book makes transformation feel both possible and practical. Rochelle blends knowledge and wisdom with grace and compassion, guiding readers to reconnect with who they truly are – not through theory, but through lived, human experience.'

— **Jenny Landgren**, Leadership Author and Behavioural Science Expert

'Learning to recognise and respond to the signs that something isn't right is at the heart of this book. Through real-life examples, Rochelle shows what happens when we ignore those signals and how to listen, take stock, and adjust in real time. Anchoring ourselves, setting boundaries, and aligning with our values creates a steady foundation that grounds us amid chaos and pressure. Each conscious choice we make from that place strengthens us and ripples into the world around us.'

— **Christine D'Mello**, Author and Coach

'A compassionate and eye-opening book that helps you recognise when coping has quietly taken over. Rochelle shows how simple pauses and honest reflection can restore clarity, strength, and joy, lessons that apply as much to life as to work.'

— **Namrata Adsul**, Project Manager and Author

'Losing oneself and one's voice is a tragedy that can be avoided. Through lived experience and deeply supportive guidance, Rochelle opens a clear path to freedom and self-trust for anyone ready to lead without losing themselves.'

— **Linda Vettrus-Nichols**, Clarity Coach and Author

'Rochelle has walked the corporate tightrope and emerged with hard-won wisdom. Her insights would have saved me years of struggle and helped me find balance sooner. This is a book for anyone who wants to succeed in demanding systems without sacrificing their health, family, or peace of mind.'

— **Ambassador Terry Earthwind Nichols**, Top 10 Thought Leader and Author

Anchored

Staying grounded when everything speeds up

ROCHELLE TROW

Rethink

First published in Great Britain in 2026
by Rethink Press (www.rethinkpress.com)

Author's disclaimer

This book draws on my own reflections and on real experiences of the many people I've worked with and learned from. While the events described are true in their essence, identifying details and names have been changed to protect privacy. The stories are shared with respect and care, in service of the insights they reveal.

For my sons, Tako and Zviko, who were born into a world that moves fast and measures worth by noise and numbers. Learn to move differently. Pause. Feel. Choose what matters to you before the world tells you what to chase. Remember that who you are beneath it all is already enough and always will be.

For everyone finding their way through this same world, I hope these words help you breathe a little easier and find steady ground again.

Contents

Foreword

What if the very qualities that make you an exceptional leader – your steadiness, intuition and humanity – are also the first to erode in a fast-moving system?

During more than twenty-five years of coaching senior executives, boards and leadership teams around the world, I have witnessed how high-performing leaders can appear wholly successful on the outside while quietly disconnecting on the inside. They deliver, perform and adapt – they seemingly function well – and yet something essential begins to thin out. Ease. Presence. Joy. The simple, yet profound, sense of being anchored in oneself.

Every leader I meet today faces the same tension: how to stay true to themselves when the pace around them keeps rising. Leaders don't need more productivity hacks; they need a way to stay whole while the world accelerates.

I first met Rochelle many years ago when she was an HR executive at a global pharmaceutical company and hired my firm, then Heimann Cvetkovic & Partners, to work with her executive team. I later became her personal executive coach. From our first encounter, I knew she was different. Rochelle observed what others missed. She could name the undercurrent beneath the conversation, not to critique, but to unlock growth. She articulated the unseen with a grounded precision that made people stop, breathe and reconsider. Few leaders embody both intelligence and humanity in equal measure. Rochelle has always carried both deeply. I am honoured to call her a former client, a long-time colleague in the work of leadership and a cherished friend.

Corporate systems are built for speed, efficiency and delivery, and while there is nothing inherently wrong with that, the system's pace too often begins to define the leader's identity. Motion replaces meaning. Composure replaces honesty. Achievement replaces aliveness. I have sat with countless leaders at the exact moment they realise the cost, when success begins to feel strangely hollow, or when they notice they are tired in a way that sleep doesn't fix.

Rochelle knows that moment intimately. She writes from lived experience, not only as someone who once pushed herself beyond her limits, but as someone who later chose to return to corporate life on her own terms, with a wiser and more grounded way of leading.

That is what makes *Anchored* so profoundly important. This book gives you a practical, immediately usable way of leading that keeps you grounded, clear and effective in the moments that matter most.

This book is not another self-help promise of balance or boundaries. It is a deeper, wiser invitation to reclaim the parts of yourself that the system will not protect. Rochelle shows you how to stay grounded while everything around you accelerates. Not by slowing the world down, but by strengthening your own inner steadiness. She reminds us that wholeness is not created for you by an organisation; it is safeguarded by attention, intention and the courage to listen inwardly even when the system rewards you for ignoring yourself.

For leaders who want to succeed in a corporate environment without losing themselves, Rochelle offers both a mirror and a path. She captures the quiet ache so many feel but rarely name: the fatigue, the pressure to keep performing, the subtle drift away from your own voice. She offers a way back to clarity, presence and the kind of leadership that feels not only effective but *true*. Her approach helps you stay clear, decisive and effective even under pressure.

What I admire most about this book is its honesty. Rochelle does not preach; she reveals. She does not position herself above the reader; she walks beside you. Through her stories, insights and gentle provocations, she gives leaders permission to pause long enough to reconnect with the wisdom they already carry. In doing so, she subtly begins to reshape how the system itself can evolve, one grounded leader at a time.

Throughout her book, Rochelle gives leaders reflective tools, honest stories and practices that bring you back to yourself. She shows you where you can lose yourself, why it happens, and how to return with more wisdom than before.

If you are holding this book, chances are you already know that something needs to shift. Not your ambition, talent or commitment, but the way you source your energy and your sense of self as you lead. Rochelle will show you that you can contribute powerfully without abandoning yourself in the process. You can move fast without losing depth. You can succeed without sacrificing what makes you human. You will walk away with strategies you can put into action immediately.

In a world that keeps speeding up, *Anchored* is a rare gift – a reminder that the most sustainable form of leadership begins not with acceleration, but with grounding. Not with striving, but with presence. Not with proving, but with remembering who you are.

This is a book every leader should read before burnout, not after it.

Settle in. Take a deep breath. Let this book offer you the pause you didn't realise you needed, and the grounding you have always deserved.

Nicole Heimann
Founder and Former Co-CEO, Heimann Cvetkovic & Partners AG, Author and Global Thought Leader in Authentic Leadership

Introduction

If you've picked up this book, my guess is that others already see you as successful. You've worked hard, earned credibility and bear the kind of responsibility that makes people look to you when it matters. They see someone steady, capable, driven. What they don't always see is the load you quietly carry. The constant rhythm of expectations, the pull to keep up and the fatigue that sometimes follows success. You've achieved so much, and yet, somewhere along the way, you've started to feel a subtle drift away from your natural rhythm. Outwardly, you seem composed, but inside, you feel stretched.

Maybe you find yourself staying quiet in meetings even though you know you have something worth saying. Perhaps you nod along to decisions that don't sit right with you, because speaking up feels risky. Maybe you're simply tired; not defeated, just weary from always being 'on'. Perhaps you miss the ease you once felt – the sense that your work and who you are still belonged in the same story.

Here's the heart of what this book offers in one line: a way to keep contributing and succeeding in fast-moving systems without losing the steadiness and humanity that make your work meaningful.

Modern work often rewards motion over meaning, composure over honesty and delivery over depth. Almost every leader I know has felt that tension – the pull to deliver and the quiet wish to feel more human while doing it.

Wholeness isn't something a system can hand you; it's something you can choose to protect and restore. Every conscious choice you make begins to reshape the system around you. Too many leaders discover this only when they've already pushed themselves too far – in the fatigue, sleepless nights, or hollowness after reaching a milestone that doesn't feel as satisfying as it should. I don't want you to wait for that breaking point. Consider this book an invitation to *pause*, look beneath the surface and choose differently.

Here's what's possible if you do: leadership that feels lighter, truer and more sustainable, where you no longer trade health for results, voice for safety, or presence for approval.

I know this tension firsthand. You can love your work and still feel the quiet cost of how the system runs. For me, it didn't happen all at once. It built slowly through long days, late nights and the subtle pressure to keep performing even when something inside was asking me to pause. I had built a career on steadiness and delivery, but somewhere along the way, that steadiness turned into survival.

I remember one meeting that made this build-up impossible to ignore. We were debating a critical decision. Privately, several executives had voiced concerns to me. Yet, when it mattered, those doubts seemingly disappeared, and silence passed for alignment. I didn't speak up either, not out of agreement, but because I was tired of carrying the unease that others avoided. Driving home that evening, a realisation landed quietly but firmly: I was not merely tired, I felt disconnected. Disconnected from my voice, from ease and from the parts of me that used to feel alive at work. I could feel the beginnings of burnout, though I didn't call it that yet.

This *awakening* isn't a single event, but the dawning awareness that you have learned to lead for the system while slowly losing touch with yourself. You have mastered performance yet drift from presence. And the cost is no longer invisible; it shows up in your body, your energy and your joy.

This book is for anyone who recognises that pattern. For people who have already proven themselves and are ready to lead with the same sense of well-being that fuels their success. For leaders who want their leadership to feel as real and human as the values that guide it. For those who care deeply about others, their purpose and the bigger picture, and who want to stay grounded in themselves.

It doesn't matter what your title is or where you work. What connects you to these pages is the quiet truth you already sense: a way to succeed that feels whole, sustainable and true to who you are.

I was born in apartheid-era South Africa into a family of humble means. Going from those beginnings, where doors were closed to people like me, to sitting at global executive tables wasn't inevitable; it was a deliberate climb driven by persistence, learning and faith in what was possible.

Over the years, I have worked in some of the world's most respected organisations, guided by exceptional mentors and coaches, and been exposed to leadership programmes that many only dream of attending. The truth is, none of that prepares you for the moment when success stops feeling sustainable. Those programmes teach you how to lead *for* the system. They offer frameworks, but not wholeness.

That's why our voices matter here: mine, yours and those of the many leaders who walk this path. Together, they trace what it means to stay whole while leading within systems that rarely pause for breath.

Unlike many leadership books, which offer steps, models or habits to master, *Anchored* won't give you a checklist. Growth is circular. You don't outgrow fear or master alignment once and for all; you return to them in new forms, again and again. *Anchored* recognises that reality. It's written for people who live and lead in motion and who don't have the luxury of stepping away to find themselves. That work happens here, in the middle of deadlines, meetings and conversations that matter.

This book isn't theory. It's a conversation and a mix of stories, reflections and gentle provocations that help you turn awareness into daily practice. You'll find reflection questions, real-life examples and simple ways to integrate what you're learning as you read. It's written to meet you where you are and walk alongside you as you begin to notice your own patterns.

There are various anchors, a self-assessment and some useful metaphors, but they're not checklists or quick fixes. They're mirrors, designed to help you see differently and make more conscious choices in the flow of real work and life. That's what makes this book different. It's not about escaping the system or fixing it; it's about seeing yourself clearly within it and leading from that position of clarity, one grounded choice at a time.

The leaders I work with often describe this shift as feeling steadier, simpler and more honest. They feel more anchored, less reactive. It's less about proving, more about being present.

If you choose to do this work, here's what becomes possible:

- **Clarity:** A way to reconnect with your values so your decisions feel aligned, not forced.
- **Confidence:** The steadiness that comes from integrity, not the fragile kind built on approval.
- **Boundaries:** The ability to protect your energy, so you stop running on empty and start showing up whole.
- **Sustainable growth:** Success that lasts, because it's rooted in who you are, not in how much you can endure.

These shifts come from a rhythm of wholeness – a daily practice of noticing, choosing and returning to what matters most.

Here's the promise: you don't need to leave to come back to yourself. You can thrive within the system, succeed on your terms and finally feel aligned with the life you've worked so hard to build. The system will take time to change, but you don't have to wait. Each anchored choice you make helps shift its rhythm from within. That's how change begins: not by waiting for a new system, but by becoming steadier within it.

PART ONE
THE PARADOX WITHIN WHICH WE LEAD

A paradox isn't a riddle. It's two truths that seem to oppose each other, but *both matter.* In modern leadership, paradox lives everywhere: the system needs results; people need renewal. You can love your work and still feel the quiet cost of how the system runs. The modern corporate world wasn't designed to make people whole. It was designed to make things work efficiently, predictably and at scale.

Real strength isn't about slowing the world down; it's about standing on strong ground while it speeds up. As Brené Brown notes in *Strong Ground* (2025), steadiness – not speed – is what lets us keep moving with purpose in the face of uncertainty.

Part One lays the foundation we'll use throughout the book. Chapter 1 names how systems shape behaviour (often before we notice), why fear and approval get reinforced, and how a well-trained ego can become both armour and identity. This isn't an argument against ambition or structure. It's an invitation to lead from steadiness within them.

1
The System Trade-Off

When I talk about the corporate system, I mean the shared design of modern organisations – the hierarchy, incentives and unspoken norms that keep productivity high and fear just beneath the surface. Although the examples in this book draw from corporate life, the same dynamics play out in any environment that measures worth and rewards speed, ranging from start-ups to hospitals and from NGOs to government offices.

Throughout this book, when I refer to 'the system,' I mean the full operating environment we now inhabit; the intertwined layers of structure, technology and culture that define modern work. It includes the business models, targets and incentives; the hierarchies and approval chains that govern decisions; and, increasingly, the digital systems and AI tools that automate judgement, accelerate pace and reshape what belonging means. These forces together create a rhythm that rewards speed, compliance and control, often at the expense of reflection, creativity and connection.

To be clear: this isn't an argument against the system. I've thrived within it, learned from it and still believe in what it can achieve when it works well. Corporate structures can mobilise brilliance at a scale no individual ever could. The problem isn't the existence of hierarchy or ambition; it's that the system changes slowly while people within it evolve more quickly. The real work is learning how to stay anchored while the system catches up – to build your own strong foundation rather than waiting for the ground to steady itself.

When I refer to our 'inner systems', I mean the human patterns – emotional, nervous and psychological – that adapt to survive inside it. The instinct to brace before a meeting. The over-preparation that keeps you from disappointing others. The quiet self-doubt that whispers, 'Don't risk it.'

I've spent over twenty-five years inside this world, working across seven global organisations spanning retail, FMCG, pharmaceuticals, consumer health, manufacturing, and semiconductors. Different industries, brands and products, but beneath the surface, the same design. The bigger the organisation, the more complex the matrix. There are layers of business units, divisions and functional hierarchies, each with competing goals, metrics and incentives. In theory, these structures create alignment and accountability. In practice, they breed tension. Sales and marketing fight for visibility, R&D and operations for resources, HR for credibility, and leaders spend as much time managing politics as they do performance. Today, that tension is amplified by technology: automation accelerates timelines, AI filters data before humans can, and decisions that once required dialogue now move at algorithmic speed. The human system hasn't evolved as quickly as the digital one, and exhaustion often lives in the gap.

As an HR executive, I wore two hats: one functional, the other business. My bonus was driven by my business unit's success, and not necessarily by the broader health of the organisation. That meant that, even when I sat at the executive table as the voice of people and culture, the commercial pressures shaped what I said – and what I stayed silent about. The same reward mechanisms that are meant to drive performance also quietly train fear: fear of losing standing, fear of being left out, fear of not belonging.

Many leaders don't choose silence out of apathy; they do it out of fear of losing credibility, security or belonging. Because behind the polished corridors and strategy slides sits an unspoken truth: the higher you climb, the narrower the space for dissent. Every voice knows the cost of being too honest. Question too much, and you risk being seen as difficult. Challenge too early, and you risk being left out of the next transformation. So the conversations grow quieter, the smiles more practised, and self-protection slowly replaces authenticity.

The system doesn't ask for this explicitly, but it's *inadvertently* engineered into its reward mechanisms. Performance ratings, pay grades, job titles and nine-box talent matrices become subtle signals of worth. Those labelled 'key talent' are given access to leadership programmes, exposure and stretch roles – the very tools that amplify visibility and ambition. Meanwhile, the majority are expected to sustain the machine from below, often with limited access to opportunities for growth or reflection. Layered on top of this now sits digital visibility – engagement metrics, productivity trackers, online presence scores – new currencies of credibility that keep the same old fear alive, just coded differently.

Over time, people learn how to navigate the system – how to present, agree and adapt *just enough* to stay safe and progress. Systems shape behaviour long before people notice. They don't just direct what we do; they teach us who to be. That's where conscious choice comes in. There's nothing wrong with climbing the ladder or seeking reward; the question is whether the climb still aligns with who you are. Ambition anchored in truth is healthy. Ambition driven by fear or approval quietly erodes you.

Whether we intend to or not, we begin to live split lives: one that performs, and one that feels. We stay visible to the organisation but invisible to ourselves. We achieve, but our inner voice grows quieter. It's a trade-off we've been conditioned to make. The same traits that enable you to thrive within the system can slowly separate you from yourself.

This is the paradox every modern leader inhabits. When I say 'leader', I mean anyone shaping outcomes, whether you manage teams, projects, households or ideas. Leadership in this context is less about position and more about presence.

The system values certainty; wholeness invites doubt. The system prizes independence; wholeness depends on connection. The system rewards endurance; wholeness calls for renewal. The system celebrates composure; wholeness requires honesty. These aren't contradictions to fix; they're tensions to hold. The first keeps the organisation alive. The other keeps the people alive.

Between these worlds stands what I call the 'ego' – not arrogance, but the part of us that builds identity around safety, control and approval. It's the voice that says, 'I'll be enough when I achieve, when I'm recognised, when I'm needed.' In the corporate world, that voice is rewarded early and often. It protects us from exclusion but also distances us from truth. It helps us survive, but it can't help us evolve. Over time, the ego becomes both armour and identity – loyal, brilliant and exhausted.

The work of conscious leadership isn't to reject the system or shame the ego; it's to bring awareness to both. To use the very insight the system gives us about scale, structure and accountability while staying honest about what it costs when we forget ourselves. This book isn't about leaving the corporate world. It's about learning to stay whole within it and meet its demands without sacrificing your own. Because the system will take time to change, our power lies in how we show up within it. When we stand on strong personal ground – values, awareness and self-trust – we set in motion a ripple that slowly shifts culture around us. Culture isn't built in off-sites or values statements; it's built in the micro-choices we make every day, how we speak up, how we recover after setbacks, and how we react when pressure rises. When those choices come from awareness instead of fear, culture changes itself.

As AI continues to transform how we work and connect, these small acts of grounded humanity matter more than ever. They're how we begin to influence the system, not by forcing it to change overnight, but by holding our own foundation steadily enough for the ripple to spread. It's true, the system can be hard to live in. It asks a lot, gives little space, and sometimes leaves us questioning whether we can stay without losing ourselves. But it is possible. The system may shape us, but it doesn't define us. What defines us is how we choose to stand grounded, aware and willing to move forward, even when the ground beneath us shifts.

This book follows the rhythm: **Notice → Anchor → Choose → Return**. It's a rhythm that helps you stay awake, steady and whole, right in the heart of the system.

It isn't a manual to master or a framework to memorise; it's a rhythm to return to – a way of noticing where you are, what you need, and how to come back when you drift. You don't need to escape the system to find yourself again. You can lead with presence, succeed on your terms and feel at home in the life you've worked so hard to build.

Think of this work as unfolding in simple cycles:

- **Connect with your values** – let values be the compass that guides tough choices.
- **Listen inwardly** – the signals you override are often the truths you need most.
- **Embody wholeness** – show up as you are; authenticity restores energy.
- **Act with integrity** – close the gap between inner truth and outer action.
- **Reclaim freedom** – not by leaving, but by staying awake and real within the system.

You'll revisit these practices throughout the book, following a pattern of noticing, anchoring, choosing and returning to what matters most.

The Wholeness Journey map

Before we dive deeper, it helps to have a reference point showing the rhythm at a glance. The Wholeness Journey map below represents a simple way to see the inner movement this book takes you through.

The terms used in the map signify the following:

- **Insight:** What this Part helps you see
- **Pull:** The emotional tension you may feel
- **Practice:** How it comes to life in reality
- **Shift:** What begins to change in you

The map isn't a framework to memorise; it's a companion you can return to whenever you lose your footing. Think of it as a compass showing where you are in the journey and what's shifting in you at each stage.

Part One – The Paradox Within Which We Lead:

- **Insight:** You can't control how fast the world moves, but you can decide where and how you stand in it.
- **Pull:** The tension between performance and presence – the system demands speed while your spirit craves steadiness.
- **Practice:** Notice the system in you – the rush, the silence, the pride that hides fatigue.
- **Shift:** Ground yourself first. Strength becomes steadiness rather than control.

Part Two – Beliefs That Make Us Survive:

- **Insight:** The patterns you learned to stay safe and succeed, even when they cost you energy or authenticity.
- **Pull:** Fear sits in the body; it drives you to over-deliver, please others and keep control.
- **Practice:** Notice how the system often rewards composure, reliability and endurance, even when they keep you small.
- **Shift:** As awareness grows, you see that these coping mechanisms once kept you safe but now quietly separate you from yourself. The cost isn't only exhaustion; it's subtle self-abandonment.

Part Three – Anchors That Help Us Thrive:

- **Insight:** Steadiness comes from awareness, boundaries and alignment.
- **Pull:** Fear is still there, but now you meet it consciously instead of letting it steer.
- **Practice:** You come home to yourself through three simple anchors:
  - – Awareness – seeing what's true.
  - – Boundaries – protecting what matters.
  - – Alignment – leading from within.
- **Shift:** Fear becomes information instead of instruction. You act out of integrity rather than defence.

Part Four – When Doubt Speaks, Wholeness Replies:

- **Insight:** After growth comes hesitation, the mind's way of testing your courage.
- **Pull:** Doubt lives in the mind; fear lives in the body. They speak over each other, one questioning your worth, the other tightening your chest.
- **Practice:** Three familiar voices appear:
  - – 'If they see the real me, they'll think I'm not enough.'
  - – 'If I draw the line, I'll lose everything I've built.'
  - – 'Better the version I know than the self I don't.'
- **Shift:** Doubt becomes discernment, a sign of expansion, not failure. Fear alerts; the mind interprets. Growth begins when both are heard.

Part Five – Thriving Within The System:

- **Insight:** Wholeness is the meeting point of the body and mind, uniting what grounds you with what guides you.
- **Pull:** Fear shows up first, doubt follows fast. When you meet both with awareness, steadiness replaces reactivity.
- **Practice:** You bring insight into motion, meeting fear differently and shaping your days around what you truly value.

- **Shift:** You learn to coexist with the system without abandoning yourself in it. Wholeness becomes a rhythm: Notice → Anchor → Choose → Return.

The three threads that run through it all:

- Fear speaks through the body.
- Doubt speaks through the mind.
- Wholeness begins when the two learn to listen to each other.

If you'd like a printable version of **The Wholeness Journey** for reflection or journalling, you can download it at rochelletrow.com.

Throughout the book, you'll also find short Research Spotlights – concise insights drawn from neuroscience, psychology, organisational studies and real-world reports that connect lived experience with wider evidence and context.

Before you leave Part One

The system will always reward what keeps it running, but wholeness begins when you start noticing what keeps *you* alive inside it. Every day brings small moments to choose awareness over autopilot, to pause before saying yes, to sense what your body already knows, and to hear the truth beneath the noise. These are the first quiet acts of reclaiming yourself.

You don't need to leave the system to find freedom. The work begins right where you are: in the tension between performance and presence and in the space between what's rewarded and what's right for you. The smallest act of awareness – a breath before a reply, a question before compliance – can change the quality of how you show up.

Before you turn the page, take a breath. Notice where the system shows up in you: in the rush to please, in the silence before a meeting or in the pride that hides fatigue. Notice what stings and what softens. These are your signals. They show you where survival still runs the show and where something in you is ready to lead differently.

In Part Two, we'll look beneath those signals to the hidden beliefs that once helped you cope but now quietly keep you small. You don't need to be tougher to thrive in demanding systems; you need to be truer. And truth always begins with noticing.

PART TWO
BELIEFS THAT MAKE US SURVIVE

Most of us don't burn out in a single blaze. We slowly erode. One unspoken no. One late-night push. One meeting where you swallow your truth to keep the peace. Day by day, you hold it together for everyone else until you realise you've drifted away from yourself amid your own success. We begin here with the quiet unravelling – the point at which success starts to cost more than it should.

Coping doesn't look like failure; it looks like professionalism. Calm in the storm. Dependable under pressure. The rewards are promotions, pay rises and a reputation for 'handling anything'. But your body keeps score – the clenched jaw, the lack of sleep, the Monday dread that starts on Sunday. These aren't flaws to fix; they're messages. Quiet reminders that something in you wants to be heard.

Part Two tells the truth of that survival – the invisible ways we learn to cope, belong and keep performing even as we thin out inside. You don't need to work at a 'bad' company to feel the weight. Most systems prize steadiness over honesty and output over awareness. Those rewards train you to stay protected long after the pressure has passed.

I'll begin by discussing how coping became my identity and what it cost me. Then we'll name the survival beliefs that keep so many of us looping the same patterns. They're not personal failings but learned adaptations – cultural and systemic scripts we've inherited, rewarded and repeated.

You'll meet the six beliefs I have seen most often, first in myself, then across three decades of corporate life, and in the leaders I coach. They show up so consistently that I built the **Wholeness at Work Self-Assessment** to help you notice where they may be shaping you. It explores four dimensions where these patterns leave their mark: **Integrity** (felt alignment), **Resilience** (recovery, not endurance), **Voice** (truth with boundaries), and **Presence** (staying connected in the moment).

This isn't a test or a quick-fix toolkit. It's a mirror. Awareness is the first repair. Until you see clearly, choice is theoretical. So, as you read, notice what stings. Which sentences do you want to skim over? That isn't weakness; it's an invitation to pay attention.

Remember: these beliefs don't live only in your mind; they live in your body. Each belief carries a kind of muscle memory – it's how your nervous system learned to stay safe in fast, demanding environments. Being able to see them isn't just changing thought patterns; it's recognising how they echo through your reactions today.

In Part One, you traced the system and the rhythm that shapes us. Now, as you enter Part Two, turn that lens inwardly. What beliefs have been holding your rhythm hostage? Notice → Anchor → Choose → Return – begin here with Notice.

Pause before you turn the page. Notice what's already shifting.

2

The Price Of Survival

We learn early how to wear the mask that earns approval – polished, capable, composed. In the corporate world, that mask is often mistaken for strength. Many of us find safety behind professional armour, showing control on the outside while concealing what feels uncertain or tender within.

People trust us because we deliver. We're called reliable, strong, a safe pair of hands. In most corporate systems, that kind of coping is treated as professionalism. We are praised for staying calm, holding it together and never letting the cracks show.

It's not just personal conditioning; the modern workplace rewards composure, predictability and control. But coping has a cost. We often mistake it for resilience, when real resilience isn't about grit or endurance – it's the ability to return to steadiness and restore ourselves.

I know this rhythm because I have lived it. For more than two decades, I built a career in corporate HR. I began in retail in South Africa, moved into HR roles in fast-moving consumer goods, and later into senior positions in global multinationals in London before relocating to Switzerland. I became the person people counted on when pressure peaked. If a project was messy, I stepped in to fix it. If conflict threatened to unravel a team, I smoothed it over. On paper, it looked like I was thriving: senior titles, international moves, a marriage, twins, holidays that seemed glamorous. A full life that others admired. Inside, I was quietly eroding.

Coping isn't weakness; it's a survival strategy that once kept us safe. The trouble starts when coping becomes our identity – a protector turned prison. It's seductive because it looks like strength. I was praised for being calm in chaos and dependable under pressure – words that once felt like medals but became weights when pinned to armour.

Coping had become my identity long before corporate life. As a child, I learned that belonging meant holding myself together, working hard and showing up positively no matter what was happening inside. Early in my career, a senior leader called me a 'rough diamond', a mix of praise and critique that left me feeling insecure.

Instead of being seen for the truth I carried, I felt judged for how I delivered it. The message I heard was clear: your insight is valuable, but only if you present it softly, more like us. So I polished harder, trying to fit a mould that might finally make me acceptable.

Psychologist Carl Jung (1959) wrote about the shift that happens when we stop seeking validation from the outside world and begin turning inwards to understand ourselves. At the time, I didn't know how to do that. I kept chasing the dream of belonging, trying harder to please others while silencing more of myself. By the time I was operating in the glass offices I once only imagined, I had become fluent in pretending.

Coping wasn't just how I survived pressure; it was the composed front that concealed a constant fear that I wasn't enough. I felt like a fraud. It was a classic case of impostor syndrome. So, I perfected the armour – the polished front I thought the system would reward. The feedback always circled back to the same refrain: 'rough diamond'. My truth might have been valid, but because I didn't package it neatly enough, it was seen as disruptive. Over time, I stopped trying to speak up. Like so many leaders, I silenced myself not out of apathy, but out of fear that honesty might cost me belonging.

Behind the polished exterior was a woman who couldn't switch off – nights spent staring at the ceiling, replaying earlier conversations, shoulders tight, breath shallow and a nervous system on constant alert. The truth? Outside of work, there was almost no capacity left for my other roles. Not for being a wife or a mother and barely for being a daughter, sister or friend. I went through the motions of having a social life, but I wasn't fully present. My mind was at work, solving problems no one else could see. My life looked full, but it felt hollow.

When people imagine burnout, they picture collapse – a dramatic resignation, a leader who can't get out of bed, a body that simply gives up. That wasn't how it was for me. Burnout wasn't a cliff. It was erosion – the slow wearing down of the self through every unspoken no. I always said yes because I didn't feel I could afford not to. Every time my nervous system flared with a trigger that ran deeper than the moment, I pushed it aside. Every time, I traded truth for approval. Each small compromise looked harmless, but together they hollowed me out.

As Arianna Huffington (2014) reminds us in *Thrive*, the constant push for achievement can trick us into believing that exhaustion is proof of commitment. I convinced myself of the same. Burnout crept in quietly, one compromise at a time. We live in a culture that applauds endurance and normalises depletion through the 'always-on' calendar, the silent rule that exhaustion equals ambition and the belief that to earn your seat at the table you must carry more than is human.

I lived on autopilot. My mind became a hamster wheel, spiralling into over-control and running constant chatter. I would walk into meetings rehearsing every possible outcome and board long-haul flights with my body already braced for the conflicts waiting on the other end. Even when I was home, my head wasn't. I didn't crash; I faded. One day I was at work, and the next, I was gone, booked off with stress.

From the outside, I still looked functional. My body worked, but inside, my mind was in overdrive. I couldn't access the simplest parts of myself – clarity, calm, even words at times. I'd stare at my laptop, unable to string thoughts together, yet still feel the pressure to perform. Because the fading was quiet, no one noticed, not even me.

The mind can explain things away, but the body doesn't. Long before I was willing to admit how much I was eroding, my body was telling the truth: the headaches; the teeth grinding; the restless legs on long flights; the fatigue that followed me into every weekend; and the extra weight that no diet seemed to shift. Physician Gabor Maté (2012) explores how the body often speaks the truths the mind refuses to face. He reminds us that symptoms aren't simply problems to fix; they're messages asking to be heard. My body wasn't failing me – it was trying to save me.

It's no wonder we're taught to trust systems – data, deadlines, deliverables – over our own cues. But the body's wisdom doesn't speak in metrics. It speaks in sensations, and I had forgotten how to listen. It wasn't that my body was breaking down; it was breaking through, forcing me to stop. The message finally came in a way I couldn't ignore. A freak accident left me with a broken wrist. Hours later, I was in surgery, which forced me to stop and sit still in a way I'd been avoiding for years. Looking back, I see it clearly: my body did what I wouldn't. It demanded I slow down and listen. The symptoms were signals. Like so many of us, I'd pulled out the batteries. I had pushed through, convinced that strength meant carrying on. But the fire doesn't go away simply because you ignore the alarms.

What unsettles me most now is not the exhaustion itself, but the way I began to disconnect within my own success. I noticed the shift gradually. I wasn't the woman I used to be. My energy for politics drained away. I had less fight to hold my ground in conflict. I told myself it was maturity, but really, I was disappearing behind the mask of composure.

While I grew quieter on the outside, the noise inside grew louder. My mind never stopped. I became more easily triggered by colleagues' behaviours – a sharp tone, dismissive glance or underhanded comment. At first, I thought it was about them, but the discomfort wasn't really theirs to carry. It was about what their actions stirred in me, and the unresolved places I hadn't yet faced. As Oprah Winfrey and Bruce D. Perry (2021) describe in *What Happened to You?*, our past experiences shape the emotional patterns that play out in the present. Understanding those roots isn't about making excuses; it's about finding explanations and gaining insight into why we think, feel and react the way we do. Those unresolved places weren't weakness; they were information. Instead of listening, I kept pushing them down, mistaking composure for strength.

From the outside, I had everything I thought I wanted: a respected career, financial security, a family and a life that seemed enviable. On the inside, I was drifting away from myself. The joy I once felt in work dimmed into duty. I became known for what I could carry, not for who I was. At home, it wasn't much different. I told myself I was tired because my marriage was failing and because I carried a heavier burden than most. I told myself this was just how life was meant to feel – always another demand waiting, another reason to override the signals within me.

Yet, something shifted when I later returned to corporate life for eighteen months. In the past, I would have softened or delayed difficult truths to be polite and stay safe. This time, I spoke plainly, naming what I saw – not with armour, but with care – and nothing broke. The difference wasn't the organisation; it was me. What gave me that confidence wasn't luck; it was the inner work of unlearning old beliefs and of building new anchors. This book explores the mindsets and practices that helped me become this steadier version of myself. If it feels far away right now, don't lose heart; the chapters ahead will walk you through the same inner shifts that helped me find my way back.

Recognising the paradox that the same systems that reward our coping can quietly strip away our wholeness is the first step towards the freedom to choose differently. It's a step towards seeing that you can look like you're thriving and still be running on empty, and that clarity and grounded honesty can exist inside the same walls that once demanded silence.

Before you turn the page, pause for a moment. Where do you recognise your own version of coping – the places you stay composed when you're actually exhausted, or the roles you keep performing long after they no longer fit? Notice what your body has been trying to tell you. The truth isn't asking you to collapse; it's asking you to listen.

3

The Illusion Of Safety

You know the cost of coping now. You've seen it in my story, and perhaps you've recognised it in your own. The harder question is, if coping wears us out so quietly, why do we keep doing it?

The answer isn't that we enjoy it. No one chooses exhaustion or invisibility. We keep doing it because we've been taught to – not by one big moment, but through thousands of small ones at home, school and work. From an early age, we absorb what earns us approval, what counts as strength and what keeps us safe. Those lessons once made sense – they were shaped by families and systems trying to protect us – but over time, they harden into 'truth'.

These beliefs aren't about possibility or faith; rather, they're protective beliefs – learned patterns that once kept us safe but now limit who we can become. They become invisible, reinforced in every performance review, offhand comment and nod of praise when we carry more than is wise. They once helped us survive, but left unexamined, they slowly thin us out.

I lived under these beliefs for decades. Now, in my coaching work, I hear them echoed in leadership meetings and offices across industries. They are delivered in different words, but the message is the same: 'This is what I thought I had to believe to succeed.'

In this chapter, I want to name those beliefs, not to shame them (they once kept you safe), but to bring them into the light. Until you can see them clearly, you can't choose differently.

Before we begin, it helps to see the terrain we're about to walk. What follows isn't theory; it's a belief-based map of how our inner systems learn to adapt and survive inside fast-paced corporate structures – the same inner systems that later in this journey shape integrity, resilience, voice and presence.

Fear lives in the body's need for certainty. It tightens the chest before a meeting and speeds the voice when silence would serve us better. It convinces us that control equals safety, that compliance protects belonging.

It takes time, support and courage to unlearn those reflexes and test new ways of being inside systems that may not welcome change at first. Some managers and cultures make that work easier; others don't. What matters is starting small – one choice, one conversation, one pause – without waiting for perfect conditions.

Ahead are six beliefs that quietly keep many of us in survival mode – patterns learned long ago that still shape how we lead today.

Belief One: Coping is strength

I learned early that if you want to be accepted, you have to hold yourself together. Don't show weakness. Don't let anyone see the cracks. At home, that looked like being the 'good one'. At school, it looked like excelling, no matter the cost. Later, in the corporate world, the same message was repeated in subtler ways. Calm under pressure was praised. Composure was rewarded. The lesson was clear: coping equals strength.

Coping begins as care – a way to stay capable and safe, a strategy that keeps belonging intact. But when it hardens into identity – when being 'the one who can handle it' becomes who you are – it stops protecting you and starts draining you. What once seemed admirable begins to hollow you from within.

Ralph, a consultant, believed this too. He had built his whole reputation on being the one people could always rely on. If a client panicked late at night, he was there. If a deadline seemed impossible, he stretched to meet it. Endless yeses became his badge of competence – proof he mattered. For a while, it worked. He was seen as dependable, hardworking and indispensable.

But by the time Ralph came to coaching, he was tired. He wasn't asking me how to deliver more. He was asking how to make what he delivered land differently. His performance seemed strong, but his presence was thin. He was in every room but rarely present. Distracted, already rushing to the next task, he was everywhere and nowhere at the same time.

Together, we experimented with boundaries. Ralph practised holding back his automatic yes. He limited his after-hours availability. He began to see that what he'd called coping was really overextension, a performance that protected his image more than his well-being.

At first, it felt like a risk. Would clients see him as less committed? Would colleagues think he wasn't pulling his weight? Although a few questioned his change of pace, and one manager even hinted it might signal complacency, Ralph held his ground. What happened was the opposite. Clients respected his clarity. Colleagues noticed he was sharper, more grounded and more present. His delivery didn't just perform; it landed.

Ralph learned what I had eventually had to learn too: the world applauds the armour, but it is presence, not performance, that represents real strength. And presence is only possible when you stop equating endurance with value.

Belief Two: Silence keeps me safe

I knew this belief well. In executive meetings, I often kept my voice steady. When I disagreed with a decision but worried how my disagreement would be received, I nodded along instead of speaking up. I told myself I was being professional, that keeping the peace was wiser than making waves. The cost of silencing myself at work showed up at the dinner table, in the quiet distance between the people who mattered most and me. The same fear that kept me agreeable in meetings followed me home, leaving me present but disconnected.

Silence begins as protection – a way to stay safe, belong and keep the peace – but over time it stops protecting us. It doesn't erase conflict; it erases us. In many organisations, the risk is real: power dynamics and culture often shape who can speak safely. That's why it helps to start small by practising using your voice in low-stakes or trusted spaces until your confidence builds. Voice isn't volume; it's alignment.

Simone, a senior HR leader in the pharmaceutical industry, lived this belief for years. Her colleagues nicknamed her the 'company sponge' because she absorbed tension, carried other people's stress and smoothed over conflicts so teams could keep moving. It earned her laughter in the corridors, but the joke covered her quiet exhaustion. When we began working together, she was depleted. 'I've spent years protecting everyone else,' she told me, 'but I don't know how to protect myself.' Saying no felt selfish. Speaking her truth felt too dangerous. So she stayed quiet, even when decisions clashed with her values.

We began implementing tiny, kind boundaries in low-stakes moments: 'I can take this, but not that,' or 'Yes, but not today.' They felt almost insignificant to her, but the ripple effects were powerful. People didn't dismiss her; they leaned in. Leaders began to notice her clarity. Colleagues started listening to her differently, with greater respect and attention.

Simone discovered what I'd once resisted myself: silence doesn't keep you safe – it makes you invisible. Speaking up, even softly, builds more trust than endless smoothing over ever could.

Belief Three: Resilience means pushing through

For years, I was praised for being 'strong'. I was the one who could stretch further, absorb more and stay calm when others wavered. I wore this ability like a badge of honour. But that wasn't resilience; it was performance dressed as resilience.

Many of us grew up with mottos like 'no pain, no gain' – messages that glorified endurance. The same logic followed us into corporate life, where those who pushed through were praised, promoted and celebrated. Somewhere along the way, resilience became confused with sheer grit. By resilience, I don't mean white-knuckle endurance. True resilience is the capacity for repair and renewal – the ability to meet challenges, recover, learn and move forward. If Belief One is about identity (being the strong one), Belief Three is about process: mistaking grit for repair. Grit keeps you pushing; resilience lets you pause and restore so you can continue from a place of strength, not exhaustion.

A senior leader I once coached embodied this belief. Admired for her stamina. She was always on, always composed, seemingly unstoppable on the outside. But when she sat across from me, she described her mind as 'noise', leading to restless nights and constantly spinning through details. Even at home, she couldn't switch off. She believed resilience meant never pausing or letting anything slip.

In coaching, we reframed the idea. Resilience wasn't about pushing through everything. It was about repair, giving her mind and body time to recover before moving on to the next demand. She began with the smallest shifts: taking a breath before answering, having a short walk between meetings and giving herself permission to pause instead of rushing. At first, she felt guilty. Pausing felt like weakness to her. But something shifted. Running on empty had made her reactive – quick to fix, slow to feel. As she slowed down, her team mirrored her steadiness. Meetings softened. Conversations deepened. She realised she was clearer, not weaker, when she paused.

She discovered what I had to face myself: endurance without renewal isn't resilience; it's a tab the body eventually presents for payment.

Belief Four: I can split work and life into buckets

We're told early on that life can be separated into neat compartments. Work–life balance becomes the phrase we chase, as if balance is a matter of keeping buckets evenly filled, work in one, family in a second, health and friendships in a third. On paper, it might sound practical, but life can't be defined into buckets. You hear it in what people say, such as, 'I can keep my personal life separate,' or 'I'm someone else at home than I am at work.' These phrases sound harmless, but they hide a deeper split – the quiet belief that we can partition our humanity and still stay whole.

I believed it for years. I convinced myself I could override myself at work and then make up for it later at home. I'd push through exhaustion during the day and expect to reset when I walked through the front door. But stress doesn't clock off when you do. It follows you – into your body, your tone of voice and the space between you and the people you love most. I came home physically present but mentally absent. My family got the leftover fragments after the day had already taken the best of me. The cost wasn't loud; it was the quiet disconnection that seeped into every room.

That's the problem with buckets: they leak. Stress absorbed in one space bleeds into others. The body carries it. Relationships absorb it. Joy gets pushed to the margins. You think you're succeeding at achieving balance, but what you're really doing is letting depletion bleed into every room.

It took me years to see that integration isn't about having equal buckets, it's about wholeness. I stopped trying to switch selves and started paying attention to how I arrived in each space. When I left work, I learned to pause before walking through the door, to let my body catch up with my life. Small rituals – a deep breath, a short walk, changing clothes slowly – became ways to reconnect. The buckets began to blend, and with them, I did too. Integration is arriving as one person, wherever you are.

Belief Five: My triggers are about others

This belief is subtle because, in the moment, it feels true. For example, when someone interrupts you in a meeting, and your chest tightens in response, it feels like the problem is their arrogance. When a leader dismisses your idea, and you feel small, it feels like the problem is their lack of respect. We convince ourselves that if the other person behaved differently, we'd be fine. I told myself that too. In meetings, every clipped tone and dismissive glance made me think, *If they changed their behaviour, I'd be fine.*

Over time, I began to see that the intensity of my reactions wasn't about them. It was about me. Their behaviour pressed on something raw that was already there – old insecurities, unresolved fears, buried stories of not being enough. That's why triggers sting so sharply. They aren't verdicts about the other person; they're mirrors, reflecting something in you that wants attention.

The cost of believing that your triggers are about other people is that you give away your power. It's possible the other person's behaviour isn't OK, and boundaries do matter, but focusing on what others do won't set you free. You will waste energy trying to manage what's outside yourself instead of turning inwards to ask what your body and mind are revealing, and what they need.

Focusing outwardly keeps you trapped in frustration. The moment you turn inwards, the trigger softens.

Naming the feeling creates space to ask a clean question, set a boundary, pause, or breathe. The room doesn't need to change for your steadiness to return.

Belief Six: Boundaries make me selfish or expendable

Many of us were raised to believe our value lies in being available. At home, that meant putting others first. At school, it meant saying yes to every request. At work, it gets reinforced when the people who never say no are praised as team players, safe hands and dependable. The unspoken lesson is clear: if you set limits, you risk rejection.

That belief ran deep for Daniel, a finance director I coached. He was known as the 'go-to' for everything – the one colleagues called when deadlines slipped or crises hit. Daniel wore his availability like armour. Underneath was a quieter truth: being needed made him feel secure. He didn't just fear letting others down; he feared being left out. His calendar was overflowing, but so was his unease. If a call came, he answered. If a deadline slipped, he stayed late. His phone never left his hand; his personal life shrank into spare minutes. He'd equated busyness with belonging for so long that quiet felt like failure.

In our work together, he tried a new approach: setting deliberate boundaries. He stopped replying to late-night messages unless they were genuinely urgent. He began scheduling short non-negotiable breaks in his calendar. At first, the moments of silence unsettled him. Without constant demands, he didn't know who he was. He feared being seen as less committed. Some did question it – one leader even wondered if he'd lost his ambition – but Daniel held his course. Results spoke louder than the number of hours worked. Gradually, the narrative began to shift. His team started solving more problems on their own. Leaders noticed his clarity and respected his focus. He began to see that boundaries didn't shrink his value; they revealed it.

Daniel discovered what I had to learn too. Boundaries don't make you selfish; they make you trustworthy. When they come from respect – for yourself, for others, for the relationship – they create safety, not distance. A single grounded yes carries more weight than a hundred fearful ones. Clarity is kindness, to you and to others.

These are the six beliefs I see most often – in myself, in the leaders I coach and in the systems we all move through. Yours may look different or carry subtler stories. What matters is noticing which patterns once kept you safe and now quietly keep you small.

We learned to cope because coping kept us safe, and later we were rewarded for it. We learned silence protected us, and later it was packaged as professionalism. We learned grit was noble and called it resilience. We learned to separate work and life into tidy compartments only to discover that stress never stays contained. We learned to look outwards when triggered and slowly realised the sting was often inside us. We learned to equate availability with value and feared that boundaries might make us expendable.

These are the cultural scripts we still live by – patterns that once kept us safe and connected, but now keep us performing instead of living. They might have helped us succeed once, but over time, they narrow who we can be. That's the paradox: the same strategies that helped us survive can slowly pull us away from ourselves. We become known for what we carry, not for who we are.

Awareness is where change begins. Naming a belief loosens its grip. Seeing these patterns clearly prepares the ground for what comes next – the anchors that rebuild integrity, resilience, voice and presence.

Before you turn the page, pause for a moment. Which beliefs still shape how you move through work or home? Which ones feel most familiar in your body? Do these six beliefs resonate, or are there others you've begun to see more clearly? That's where return begins, with awareness steady enough to choose differently.

4 The Mirror To Awareness

Awareness is powerful, but in systems built for performance, it often gets sidelined. It's one thing to recognise yourself in the stories and beliefs we've named so far. It's another to pause and ask how deeply they have taken root in you? That question matters. Without it, the drift continues.

We tell ourselves we'll rest 'after this quarter', that life will feel easier 'once the pressure eases', or that we'll finally slow down when things 'settle'. But life doesn't pause on its own – systems reward motion, not reflection, which is why you must create your own pause. Without deliberate pauses, we slip back into coping, working harder yet feeling further from ourselves. Reflection interrupts that drift. It hands back choice. Awareness sounds simple, but it's not straightforward.

Seeing the pattern is one thing; staying alive to it in real time is another. It takes practice and patience before new habits take hold.

Looking in the mirror isn't easy. It asks for honesty that most of us were never taught. We rush, we rationalise, we point outwards – to the system, our workload, the timing – because it's safer than turning inwards. Avoidance isn't weakness; it's protection – the body's way of keeping us safe until we're ready to see. That's why compassion matters. When you finally pause long enough to see the truth, it can sting. But the sting isn't failure; it's your signal that awareness is landing.

In Chapter 11, you'll find the **Wholeness at Work Self-Assessment**. The assessment isn't a test or another performance metric; it's a mirror. A mirror that helps you notice three simple things: where you're steady, where you're coping, and where you may already be running low.

It looks at four dimensions that together shape your wholeness: Integrity, Resilience, Voice and Presence. These aren't abstract ideas; they're the opposites of protective mode, illustrating what steadiness feels like when you're no longer living from a place of defence.

At this stage, there's nothing to complete or score, only an invitation to notice how each dimension already shows up in you. These next pages simply offer a preview: short reflections that help you sense the dimensions before the deeper work later on.

Dimension One: Integrity – living in alignment

When integrity is steady, your yes *means* yes. Your decisions reflect your values, even under pressure. People know what you stand for, and you feel settled – not split – about the way you succeed. When integrity erodes, the cracks show. You nod in meetings while your stomach twists. You compromise too often and tell yourself it's just part of the job. That quiet friction between what you value and what you perform becomes hard to ignore. I know that feeling. Each time I smiled though I was unsettled, choosing approval over truth, I drifted further from myself.

One senior executive I worked with described leaving meetings feeling 'like I'd sold myself cheap'. On paper, he made pragmatic decisions, but the quiet cost was a growing distance between what he stood for and what he allowed. Over time, that gap didn't just steal his energy; it stole his sense of self.

REFLECTION PROMPT

Where in your week do you nod along while a quieter part of you is saying no?

Dimension Two: Resilience – more than grit

We often mistake resilience for grit, the drive to carry more weight without breaking. True resilience isn't endurance; it's repair and renewal. When resilience is steady, recovery becomes part of your rhythm. You can step away without guilt. Your body feels energised more often than depleted. You know how to pause, reset and return.

When resilience erodes, exhaustion becomes your norm. You wear tiredness like a badge of honour. Even when you stop working, your mind doesn't. Your body tells the truth with headaches, irritability or fatigue – messages you learn to override. Resilience begins the moment you start listening again.

I used to believe that resilience meant keeping everything going. But resilience without restoration isn't resilience; it's depletion in disguise. One client described resilience as 'never letting anything slip', but her body told another story – tight shoulders, restless nights, constant alertness. When she began to pause, even briefly between meetings, her team mirrored her calm. Presence, not pressure, became her new signal of strength.

REFLECTION PROMPT

What does your body do when you've been pushing too long? What's the first signal you usually dismiss?

Dimension Three:
Voice – speaking truth without apology

Voice is about truth and boundaries – the meeting point between honesty and care. When your voice is steady, you can speak up in difficult rooms. You can say no without guilt. You can be open without fear that it will be used against you. People know where you stand. When voice erodes, silence takes over. You swallow your instincts to keep the peace. You confuse being nice with being honest. You stay quiet because it feels safer, but silence slowly makes you fade from view. For years, I mistook silence for maturity, believing measured restraint was wisdom. It took time to see that silence didn't protect me; it erased me.

One client, a finance director, described herself as having 'perfect attendance but zero presence'. When she began adding just one clear sentence per meeting – 'I see it differently' – people leaned in. Her words changed little at first, but her presence did. Her influence grew as her voice returned.

REFLECTION PROMPT

Where are you still swallowing your words, and what truth is waiting underneath?

Dimension Four: Presence – staying grounded in the moment

Presence is your ability to stay connected to yourself, even under pressure. When your presence is steady, you bring calm into stressful spaces. You pause before reacting. You stay connected even when conversations get heated. People experience you as steady and real. Composure isn't the problem; it is only hollow when it becomes performance instead of connection. When presence erodes, autopilot takes over. You may look composed, but inside, you've checked out. You confuse shutdown with calm. For years, I mistook control for calm, maintaining composure that hid distance rather than created trust.

One operations leader I coached did the same. He prided himself on being 'the calmest in the room', but his team quietly admitted they never knew what he really thought. When he began practising presence – simply pausing to feel his breath before speaking – his calm shifted from detachment to connection. His influence grew because people could finally feel him land.

REFLECTION PROMPT

When do you confuse being 'calm' with being absent?

Awareness doesn't fix everything, but it does the most important thing – it gives you choice. Choice is what prepares you for the next step, which is meeting fear not as an enemy but as information you can work with. You've begun to see clearly; next comes learning how to stay that way.

Before you turn the page, pause. What did this mirror reveal? Where are you steady, where are you coping, and where might you be running low? What surprised you most? That's usually what needs your attention next.

Before you leave Part Two

You've just walked through the hardest beginning: telling the truth about survival. In Chapter 2, you saw how coping looks like professionalism on the outside but quietly drains you from the inside. In Chapter 3, you named the protective beliefs – not personal flaws, but learned strategies that once helped you belong and stay safe – that keep so many of us stuck in that cycle. In Chapter 4, you held up a mirror to notice where those patterns have taken root in you and how they may still shape your choices today.

The purpose of Part Two wasn't to fix anything; it was to help you see. To stop rehearsing old stories long enough to notice where they no longer serve you. Awareness is the first act of freedom, and now you have it.

Pause and take in what has landed. Notice what stings. Notice what makes you feel lighter after naming it. Those signals are your compass. Your mind recognises the truth, and your body confirms it. When your breath settles or tension releases, that's awareness taking root – proof that seeing differently changes more than just thought; it shifts something inside you.

And remember: disruption is not the end. It's the beginning. What you've unearthed now needs something steady to hold it. That's where we turn next. You've seen how the system rewards survival and silence, but you've also seen what it costs. You don't need to be harder, faster or stronger. You don't need more armour. What you need are anchors – the practices that bring you back. Anchors don't protect you from the storm; they keep you steady within it. In Part Three, we'll explore nine anchors and how they help you translate awareness into steadiness.

PART THREE

ANCHORS THAT HELP US THRIVE

In fast-moving systems, it's easy to drift away from what's real. Part Three is about coming home – translating awareness into rhythm and reflection into action. Authenticity isn't about proving who you are; it's about returning to what's true beneath the performance.

We're moving now from awareness to anchoring – from naming survival patterns to practising steadiness. In Part One, you explored the system; in Part Two, you uncovered the beliefs that keep you coping. That awareness is powerful, but it lives mostly in the mind. Anchoring brings it into the body, turning insight into muscle memory.

When the world pulls you back into busyness, triggers flare, or your body signals distress, you need something steady to return to. These anchors offer that steadiness. Together they form the rhythm 'Notice → Anchor → Choose → Return' – a cycle that helps you move from protection to presence.

I call the nine anchors the **Anchors of Wholeness**, and they are drawn from my own journey and the journeys of those I've walked alongside. They help you recentre your nervous system so that mind and body work together again. Anchors don't erase storms or silence doubt; they hold you long enough to remember who you are so that you can choose from a state of steadiness.

The anchors represent invitations to meet yourself where you are, reminders of the steadiness already within you. You'll explore the nine anchors across three themes:

- **Awareness:** Notice the noise, listen to your body, take the pause.
- **Boundaries:** Protect your energy, say what matters, let yourself be seen.
- **Alignment:** Make space for possibility, let your values lead you, be all of you.

Together, these anchors help you move from reflection into aligned action.

I didn't practise all nine at once. Awareness came first, then boundaries, and finally alignment – each layer teaching steadiness over striving.

Think of what follows as a conversation, not a curriculum. Begin small, with one anchor and one simple practice repeated often. Let it be felt, not forced. If you drift, you haven't failed; you can simply return. Notice resistance – it often marks the edge of growth. Make it yours; the most powerful anchor is the one you'll actually use.

Each anchor ends with cues as to what it looks like when you drift, and what it looks like when you return. They're not prescriptions, but rather patterns I've seen in myself and others. Even one is enough to notice where you lose steadiness and how to return. Your body will show you which cues matter most; trust those signals over the story your mind tells.

You'll also meet leaders whose stories bring these anchors to life. Their experiences aren't blueprints; they're signposts. Take what resonates and leave what doesn't.

Remember, none of us is perfect. Anchoring is about how quickly and kindly you return. By beginning here, you've already taken the first step back to yourself. The system may take time to change, but how you anchor within it is always yours to choose. What follows are simple, human ways of remembering yourself when the world won't slow down.

Think of what follows as a conversation, not a curriculum. Begin small, with one anchor and one simple practice repeated often. [illegible] will not [illegible] if you [illegible] for a day or two; you can simply return. Notice resistance—it often marks the edge of growth. [illegible] yours; the most powerful anchor is the one you'll actually use.

Each anchor ends with cues as to what it looks like when you[illegible] [illegible] when you return. These are not prescriptions [illegible] [illegible] [illegible] [illegible] [illegible] [illegible] [illegible] the [illegible] your mind [illegible].

You [illegible] find [illegible] which [illegible] [illegible] [illegible] [illegible] [illegible] [illegible] [illegible] [illegible].

Remember: none of this is perfect[illegible] [illegible] how quickly and kindly you return [illegible] [illegible] [illegible] [illegible] [illegible] [illegible] [illegible] [illegible] [illegible] [illegible] [illegible] [illegible] [illegible] [illegible] [illegible] [illegible] [illegible] [illegible] down.

5

Awareness: Seeing What's True

The first cluster of anchors is about noticing. In systems that prize performance over presence, noticing becomes a quiet act of return – a way of coming home to yourself before the system pulls you into who you believe you should be. When you're under pressure, your default is performance. You speed up. You deliver. You cope. On the surface, it seems to work, but beneath the surface, you begin to disconnect from yourself. Awareness interrupts the disconnection. It offers a breath before autopilot takes over, presenting a moment that returns you to choice.

These three anchors may sound simple, but they've carried me and many of my clients back to wholeness in moments when the world asked for something else:

1. Notice the noise.
2. Listen to your body.
3. Take the pause.

They're not rules; they're reminders or invitations to return to yourself when the pull to perform is strongest. Each helps you stay whole within systems that rarely slow down for your humanity.

Anchor One: Notice the noise

In systems that reward intellect and speed, the first signals to be ignored are often the ones in your head.

Ralph, a consultant at a big global firm, used to live entirely from the neck up. His days were stacked with back-to-back meetings, his nights filled with unfinished conversations running through his mind. Before and after every meeting, he rehearsed and replayed the same stories. 'If I can think through every outcome,' he told me, 'nothing can go wrong.' But what he called diligence had become draining. The more he tried to control through thought, the less space he had for presence.

One Friday evening, he caught himself drafting an email for the third time, chasing the perfect phrasing while his dinner grew cold. His partner asked a simple question, 'Are you even here?' and he didn't have an answer. That was the moment he realised how loud the noise had become.

Through coaching, Ralph began to slow the loop. He practised naming it – 'I'm rehearsing again' – and stopped treating every request as a crisis. When a client asked for an impossible turnaround, he said, 'We can do this well by Tuesday, or send a high-level draft sooner.' The world didn't collapse. Clients respected the boundary, and his team exhaled in relief. His head grew quieter.

At first, the quiet felt foreign. His mind kept rushing to fill it – refreshing his email, checking Teams' messenger, anything to prove he was still useful. But each time he caught the urge and paused, the grip loosened a little. That small shift – noticing the noise instead of fighting it – became his first act of awareness.

The noise was a signal showing where fear or fatigue had blurred into performance. As he took time to pause, his presence deepened, and his credibility grew with it. The system didn't slow down, but his awareness made space – a pause inside the noise, enough to choose differently.

What it looks like when you don't notice	*What it looks like when you do notice*
• You replay conversations instead of listening to the one you're having. • Preparation replaces presence, so people perceive you as distracted. • Your voice tightens, and your authority fades. • You leave interactions feeling drained, without knowing why.	• You catch the loop quickly: 'I'm rehearsing again.' • You prepare focused on purpose, not every paragraph. • You land more strongly because people feel your presence, not your performance. • You recover faster after tough conversations because you don't keep replaying them.

When you catch the loop starting, pause and name it out loud or on paper: 'This is fear, fatigue or the pressure to prove.' Naming turns noise into data. Then ask yourself what you need right now – a breath, a stretch or a small renegotiation. Even one conscious act resets your system.

Noise isn't the enemy; it's information. When you notice it, you lead from a place of clarity. When you ignore it, the loop and the system lead you. Over time, those small pauses begin to quieten the wider noise, too. Meetings slow down, clarity rises, and the steadiness you model starts to change what feels normal around you.

PAUSE TO REFLECT

- Where in your week do you notice the loudest noise in client demands, team dynamics or in your own head?
- When the loop starts, do you fuel it by rehearsing, or do you pause and take notice?
- If you treated the noise as a signal, not a verdict, what small shift could you make in how you show up?

Before we move on to the next anchor, notice how this research comes to life in practice and what it looks like when a leader caught in constant mental noise begins to quieten the mind and reconnect with presence instead of performance.

RESEARCH SPOTLIGHT:
When the Mind Won't Switch Off

Most leaders I've worked with know the feeling of lying awake at night, running conversations through their heads. They call it preparation and professionalism, but psychologists suggest it can also be mental overactivation – the mind rehearsing instead of resting.

Behavioural scientist Ethan Kross (2021) describes this inner loop as 'chatter' – the relentless mental noise that steals clarity. His research shows that when people repeatedly revisit painful moments, their stress response stays heightened. When they gain a little psychological distance, seeing the event as if it is happening to someone else, the body settles more quickly. Rumination doesn't protect us; it keeps the nervous system on alert long after the moment has passed.

This has a cost for leadership. Research by Nolen-Hoeksema et al. (2008) shows that repetitive, self-focused thought not only deepens distress but also depletes the mental bandwidth needed for problem-solving and self-regulation. In simple terms, when the chatter is loud, there's less room for listening, regulating and leading. A leader may still deliver the slide deck or hit the deadline, but their presence feels thin. People feel the static.

Neuroscience helps explain why. Rumination activates the brain's default mode network – the circuitry linked with self-referential worry. When this network loops, the prefrontal cortex, which governs logic and choice, is less available (Kross, 2021). The very part of the brain you need most in tense moments can be temporarily hijacked by rehearsal and regret.

Studies on decision fatigue suggest that mental energy spent replaying or pre-empting conversations gradually erodes clarity through the day. The noise doesn't just distract you; it drains the focus needed for the choices still ahead.

The hopeful news is that chatter can be interrupted. Research in emotional regulation shows that even small shifts, such as third-person self-talk or brief journalling, create distance and restore perspective

(Kross, 2021). These simple acts lower the volume enough for awareness and steadiness to return.

For leaders, the implication is clear. Quietening the chatter isn't indulgence; it's part of sustaining credibility and calm authority. When the noise rules, influence thins. When attention returns, presence strengthens. Clarity is what people trust most in those who lead them.

Anchor Two: Listen to your body

In systems that prize intellect and speed, the body becomes the most ignored instrument, yet it holds the wisdom we most need. If the mind whispers, the body speaks loudly. Stress doesn't live in your head; it lodges in your shoulders, your jaw and your gut. The headaches. The fatigue. The Sunday heaviness in your chest. Most of us are trained to override those signals, silencing them with caffeine, medicating them with painkillers or dismissing them as 'part of the job'.

I did this for years, brushing each small signal aside until, one day, a freak accident stopped me cold. A broken wrist, surgery, titanium plates and weeks of forced stillness – what felt like bad luck was really a reckoning. My body had been whispering for years, 'If you won't pause, I'll make you pause.' As physician and author Gabor Maté (2012) reminds us, stress that's hidden or ignored always finds a voice, often through the body. What I'd dismissed as minor inconveniences were really signals for attention, and when I ignored them, my body spoke louder.

Ana, a senior leader I coached, lived this same pattern. Her body was her meeting room – heart racing even while sitting still, breath shallow, jaw locked. Sleep came in fragments; she began her mornings already tired. Tension headaches, clenched muscles and fatigue that no holiday could fix. She thought resilience meant pushing through, but her body was quietly calling for care.

We began small, with her taking a breath before answering or a short walk between meetings and naming the tightness instead of swallowing it. At first, she felt guilty; pausing felt indulgent, almost unsafe. Slowly, the signals changed: the headaches eased, sleep improved, and she started waking without that feeling of dread.

Her team mirrored her calm. Meetings grew less frantic and conversations more grounded. Resilience stopped meaning grit; it became repair. As her body softened, so did her leadership. Strength stopped living in tension and started living in presence.

Across executive teams, I saw the same culture: double-hatted roles, relentless travel, silent expectations to always be on. Ignoring your body wasn't resistance; it was the currency of belonging – a costly currency that trades connection for compliance.

It can be as simple as one small tell. A client once laughed when I asked how he knew he was stressed: 'Because I stop drinking water.' Something so basic, but it was his clue. It speaks its own language in everybody: a clenched jaw, a tight stomach, a shallow breath – these are fluencies we can relearn. Learning yours is one of the first leadership skills no one teaches. The question is whether you're listening.

Organisations will always set demands that tempt you to override your limits – travel, double-hatting, endless priorities. Only you can choose to listen before you reach the point where your body insists on rest. No system will hand you permission. Listening is leadership – your responsibility and your strength. When you model that attention, others begin to trust that pace. Presence becomes contagious.

What it looks like when you don't listen	*What it looks like when you do listen*
• You override fatigue with caffeine and call it resilience. • You treat pain or tension as inconveniences instead of signals. • You confuse pushing through with being strong, while those around you absorb the strain. • You lose clarity because your body is in protection mode.	• You notice stress in your body and name it before it spirals. • You build in resets, breaths, drinking water and movement instead of pushing through. • You regulate yourself, and others mirror your steadiness. • You act from grounded presence rather than from adrenaline.

Pause once today and scan your body from head to toe. Where is the tension? Name it – jaw, shoulders, stomach, breath? Don't rush to fix it. Let awareness shape your next choice, even if it's just slowing your pace for a moment. A single conscious breath can become the hinge between depletion and repair. Over time, that simple act of listening ripples outwards: teams match your pace, meetings soften, and culture slowly recalibrates from adrenaline to attention. When leaders listen to their bodies, organisations learn to breathe again.

PAUSE TO REFLECT

- Where does stress live in your body?
- What is it trying to tell you?
- What one small signal could you begin noticing sooner before it becomes a shout?
- How might listening to your body change the way you lead, not just how you feel?

Before we move on to the next anchor, notice how this research comes to life in practice and what it looks like when a leader begins to listen to the body's early signals and learns to lead from awareness instead of adrenaline.

RESEARCH SPOTLIGHT:
When Your Body Speaks First

For years, the corporate world has rewarded people who override their body's signals. They push through fatigue. Ignore the tight chest. Quieten the lump in the throat. The story goes that resilience is about enduring. But research across psychology, neuroscience and medicine reveals a different truth: the body remembers what the mind dismisses, and eventually, it speaks.

Neuroscientist and psychiatrist Bessel van der Kolk (2015) describes how unprocessed stress can leave measurable traces in the body. Imaging studies show that prolonged stress keeps the brain's alarm system highly active while the regions that help regulate and calm it become less responsive. In simple terms, when the nervous system learns to expect a threat, the body stays on alert even when conditions are safe. Many leaders experience this as walking into a meeting already braced for impact.

Gabor Maté (2012) offers a complementary perspective, suggesting that long-term emotional suppression and unresolved stress often correlate with physical strain. He cautions against assuming direct causation, yet decades of evidence indicate that sustained tension influences how the body regulates stress and immunity.

There's also hopeful evidence. A five-week study comparing daily physical activity, mindfulness and paced breathing found that each approach reduced stress and improved sleep and mood (van der Zwan et al., 2015). The takeaway: brief, self-directed practices can help the nervous system reset.

Ignoring the body can narrow leadership presence. When you're stuck in a fight-or-flight rhythm, you're more likely to react fast, misread a tone or push ahead without listening. By contrast, leaders who attend to early bodily signals gain useful warnings – the clenched jaw before the sharp email, the restless foot before the rash decision. Listening creates a pause, a small window in which to choose differently.

The science is clear: chronic stress reshapes the body's regulation systems, yet recovery begins the moment you listen. Resilience isn't about endurance; it's about attention – noticing and responding to what the body already knows. Your body isn't an obstacle to leadership; it's your most honest ally.

Anchor Three: Take the pause

In systems that equate speed with competence, pausing can feel like resistance. Yet it's pausing that restores presence and clarity. If the head holds noise and the body gives signals, the pause is the moment you choose what to do with both. The quicker the answer, the more impressive you look, but speed often comes at the expense of clarity and presence. And systems reinforce it. Promotions go to the quick thinkers. The first hand raised gets rewarded. Leaders who slow down to reflect are sometimes labelled indecisive. The culture whispers: if you want to belong, don't pause – perform.

Ralph, a senior consultant, learned this through experience. Every ping of his phone felt like proof he mattered. Clients emailed at 8pm, and he replied within minutes. Colleagues asked for input, and he jumped in before they'd even finished the question. His speed looked like commitment, but it quietly drained his authority.

In coaching, we tried something simple but uncommon: silence. Taking a single breath or counting to ten before responding. The first time he did it, a client actually leaned in closer, waiting. In that moment, his pulse spiked. The silence felt endless, every second stretching his nerves. Part of him wanted to fill it, to prove he still had control, but he stayed with it. That moment of space landed deeper than any quick reply. Over time, people started listening more. His words carried more weight because they no longer had to compete with noise.

As Daniel Goleman (2015) notes, a brief pause can shift you from reaction to choice. That's what Ralph discovered – speed wasn't strength; awareness was. I learned it, too. The emails I regret most weren't the ones I delayed; they were the ones I sent too quickly. The agreements I regretted weren't those I sat with; they were the ones I rushed into. The system taught me speed; the pause taught me steadiness.

One client in pharmaceuticals tested the same practice during tense leadership meetings. What began as ten seconds of silence slowly changed the room. Conversations softened, better ideas surfaced and stillness became a shared signal that presence mattered there. The pause spread.

Taking the pause doesn't mean paralysis or overthinking. It means allowing yourself one breath of truth before performance takes over – a moment where ego softens and awareness leads. The culture of speed won't slow itself down. Corporate life will always reward the quickest answer, but the pause is yours to take. No one else can create that moment of space. Each pause is an act of conscious leadership – a quiet refusal to trade depth for display.

What it looks like when you don't pause	*What it looks like when you do pause*
• You say yes before you've checked your capacity and end up overloaded. • You fill silence because it feels safer than stillness. • You respond quickly, but people trust you less because your answers feel reactive. • You feel valued for speed, but not always for substance.	• You create a moment of space for values to surface before words do. • Your words carry more weight because they arrive with steadiness. • Others experience you as clear, available and trustworthy. • You begin shaping culture, showing that reflection is not hesitation; it's leadership in motion.

Pause before your next meeting and count silently to three before speaking. Notice how the room shifts and how your words land differently. You may find others begin to pause, too. Over time, those brief silences start to rewrite the culture. The tempo in meetings slows. Reactions turn into reflection. What begins as your personal pause becomes a collective one – proof that presence is contagious.

PAUSE TO REFLECT

- Think back to your last difficult conversation. What might have shifted if you had taken just one pause?
- Where in your week do you feel most pressured to equate speed with value?
- How would it feel to test the opposite by slowing down, even slightly, to let presence lead instead of performance?

Before we move on to the next anchor, notice how this research unfolds in daily leadership and what it looks like when a single pause shifts a conversation, a decision or an entire team's rhythm.

RESEARCH SPOTLIGHT:
When a Pause Changes Everything

In high-pressure environments, leaders are often rewarded for speed, quick responses, instant decisions and fast pivots. Yet emerging neuroscience shows something quieter: the most effective actions often begin with a pause.

As Daniel Goleman (2015) explains, pausing isn't a soft skill; it's a neurological reset. Under pressure, the brain's amygdala – our internal alarm system – reacts milliseconds faster than the rational prefrontal cortex. This sequence, often called an amygdala hijack, primes us to fight, flee or freeze. When unchecked, we react impulsively, firing off emails we regret, shutting down dissenting voices or doubling down on flawed assumptions.

Here's where the pause helps. Even a few seconds of intentional breathing or silence can calm the amygdala's response and give the prefrontal cortex time to re-engage (Goleman, 2015). In practice, the pause gives logic, empathy and perspective a moment to catch up.

A meta-analysis of mindfulness-based interventions found significant reductions in emotional reactivity and improved executive function (Keng et al., 2011). This growing evidence supports what many leaders already sense: silence isn't empty – it's the brain's bridge from reaction to response.

The pause also changes perception. Studies show that leaders who pause before answering are often rated as more thoughtful and trustworthy. Teams interpret the space not as hesitation, but as care. In noisy systems, the one who takes a breath often recentres the room.

Pausing isn't withdrawal or indecision; it creates micro-moments where choice can return.

Psychiatrist Viktor Frankl (2006) called the space between stimulus and response 'where freedom lives' – a truth now echoed by neuroscience, which shows that awareness restores access to choice.

For leaders, the application is simple. Embedding small rituals – a breath before speaking, a count to three before replying to an email, a moment of silence before a decision – helps prevent reactive spirals. These practices don't slow you down; they steady you. They build the muscle of awareness so that presence can lead performance. The pause isn't absence; it's choice in motion – the quiet act that turns pressure into perspective.

Before you turn the page, remember that in systems that reward speed and certainty, awareness is what slows the spin. It's how you come back to yourself before performance takes over. Awareness makes leadership possible. Without it, pressure leads you; with it, you lead yourself.

Noticing the noise. Listening to your body. Taking the pause. These three anchors don't just change how you feel; they change how others experience you. They restore presence in rooms that mistake motion for progress.

You can't stop the world from demanding more. You can't silence pressure. But you can take notice before disappearing inside it. Noticing is your first act of self-leadership – the bridge between reaction and choice. Once you notice, you begin to return.

Awareness doesn't erase the noise, the strain or the pace, but it keeps you from being swept away by them. It turns survival into self-trust. That choice – to notice, to pause, to return – becomes the quiet foundation of every other anchor that follows. Because awareness is what steadies you long enough to choose how you'll meet the world next.

6
Boundaries: Protecting What Matters

In systems that mistake availability for value, boundaries are how you stay connected. If awareness is about noticing, boundaries are about protecting. Without them, you can spread yourself too thinly and find yourself being present everywhere but grounded nowhere. You carry more than you can hold. You say yes when your body is quietly signalling no. You end up being known for what you absorb, not for who you are. Boundaries aren't walls. They don't push people away. They're bridges that let you meet others without losing your footing. They're the invisible lines that protect your energy, make your yes trustworthy and allow your presence to land.

This cluster of anchors offers three invitations:

1. Protect your energy.
2. Say what matters.
3. Let yourself be seen.

They're not about becoming hard, distant or self-centred. They're about staying whole in systems that reward overextension and call it strength.

Anchor Four: Protect your energy

In systems that celebrate self-sacrifice, protecting your energy is an act of quiet leadership. Energy is your most limited resource, and without boundaries, it can leak out through a hundred small concessions.

I know this pattern too well. For years in HR, I prided myself on being the one who could hold it all. If conflict flared up, I calmed it. If leaders clashed, I absorbed the tension. If a team was stretched, I picked up the slack. It looked like strength, but inside, I was drained. I was available to everyone but myself. I gave everyone else protection, but none to myself. The applause was constant, but so was the fatigue.

Simone, a senior leader in pharmaceuticals, lived the same story. She laughed that colleagues called her the 'company sponge', but the humour barely disguised her fatigue. 'I've spent my career protecting others,' she admitted, 'but I don't know how to protect myself.' To her, saying no felt risky. She feared boundaries would make her replaceable. So she kept saying yes, even when her plate was full. The turning point came on a Friday evening when her child asked, 'Mum, are you working again?' and she realised she had no answer that didn't sound like an apology.

The following Monday, she tried something new: the small phrase, 'I can do this, but not that.' Her voice shook the first time she said it. She half-expected a frown or a sigh, proof that her worst fear was true. Instead, the room stayed calm, and she realised most of the pressure to say yes lived in her own head.

At first, it felt awkward, almost trivial, and the effect was gradual. People didn't see her as selfish; they saw her as being clear. Colleagues stopped flooding her inbox with last-minute asks. Leaders began to hear her voice, rather than just relying on her capacity. Her presence gained weight because she'd stopped disappearing under the load.

As burnout researchers Christina Maslach and Michael P. Leiter (2022) explain, burnout is best understood as a relationship with work – a pattern of ongoing mismatches that slowly drains people over time. Boundaries help correct those mismatches before they become disconnection. At first, those shifts can look like performance dips – fewer late nights, slower replies – but over time they build deeper trust and steadier results.

The problem isn't that people like Simone or me weren't strong enough. The problem is that the system rewards over-giving and undervalues rest to the point where there's nothing left. That pattern shows up everywhere, not just in HR. Any role caught between caring for people and delivering results feels the same squeeze. The unspoken rule is clear: carry more or risk being seen as less committed. The shift wasn't that Simone or I stopped helping; it's that we learned to contribute without exhausting ourselves. The hardest part wasn't drawing the line; it was believing we were still enough once we did. Boundaries didn't make us smaller; they made us steadier.

That's something we rarely name in corporate life: everyone walks into work with a backstory. For some, that history makes them even more vulnerable when boundaries blur. Yet systems often pretend strength is endless. But strength without renewal becomes self-abandonment. What's really needed is support – not just another wellness programme, but structures that fit human limits. Leaders who remember that people are whole human beings, not just roles. Structures that don't keep piling on work and calling for resilience.

Even when you know how important boundaries are, holding them takes courage, especially when the system keeps pushing against them. The organisation may pile on more than is humanly sustainable, but only you can decide what you absorb. Boundaries don't start with policy; they start with presence. Protecting your energy isn't withdrawal; it's stewardship – the conscious act of preserving what allows you to lead at all.

What it looks like when you don't protect your energy	*What it looks like when you do protect your energy*
• You answer emails at midnight because you're afraid not to. • You agree to 'just one more project' even though you're already stretched. • You leave meetings with everyone else feeling lighter, but you feel heavier. • You find yourself the go-to shock absorber for everyone else's conflict or stress. • Your weekends become recovery zones instead of spaces for living.	• You name your capacity honestly and consistently. • You trust that saying no won't make you less valuable; it will make your yes matter more. • You stop confusing exhaustion with commitment. • Others begin stepping up because you've stopped carrying their load. • You recover faster because you no longer pour from an empty cup.

Before saying yes to the next request, pause and add one honest qualifier: 'Yes, but here's what I'd need to make it sustainable'; 'Yes, but this is what would need to shift'; 'Yes, but not now. Here's when I can.'

These small phrases shift the conversation from silent absorption to visible clarity. They teach the system how to meet you halfway. Over time, those tiny recalibrations do more than protect you; they begin to *rebalance* the culture. The more leaders hold their energy with integrity, the less burnout becomes a badge of honour. Capacity becomes contagious; balance becomes believable. When one person steadies, it gives quiet permission for others to do the same.

PAUSE TO REFLECT

- Where in your week are you saying yes out of fear rather than alignment?
- What's one place, even a small one, where you could begin protecting your energy differently?
- What story are you still telling yourself about what makes you valuable, and what if that story is ready to change?

Anchor Five: Say what matters

For years, as the HR voice in senior meetings, I saw the situation play out the same way. Before a meeting, colleagues would stop by my office to share their concerns – the doubts they'd never voice in the room. I'd walk into the meeting carrying those conversations, believing it was my job to raise what others wouldn't – and I did. But when I spoke up, the silence was deafening. My pulse raced. The air felt thick. I heard my voice tremble as I finished the sentence and waited for agreement, for eye contact, for anything. Instead, papers shuffled.

Someone cleared their throat. The moment passed. The same people who'd agreed privately looked down at their notes.

Over time, I noticed what that silence did to me. I started holding back, too. I told myself it was professionalism – that keeping the peace mattered more than making waves. Underneath was something harder to admit – fear. Fear of judgement, dismissal and being seen as difficult. Eventually, I joined the silence I had once tried to challenge. I saw the same pattern everywhere – steady, capable leaders swallowing truth to protect belonging. On the surface, they looked composed. Underneath, they were carrying an unspoken weight.

One client who worked in banking described it clearly. In meetings, everyone nodded along. In the corridors afterwards came the whispers: 'I don't think this will work,' or 'We're heading in the wrong direction.' Outwardly, alignment looked neat; underneath, mistrust grew. Decisions slowed because no one trusted the room enough to tell the truth.

Amy Edmondson's (2019) research demonstrates that when people believe they can speak up without fear of punishment or humiliation, they share ideas more openly, and collective performance strengthens. Her work defines psychological safety as a shared belief that it's safe to take interpersonal risks – a condition that allows trust and innovation to grow. Silence may offer short-term protection, but over time, it erodes confidence and weakens the very systems we depend on.

That tension was most visible at the executive table. Many leaders were double-hatted, wearing their functional role on one hand and their business leadership role on the other. The duality created pressure. It feels lonely when you're the only HR voice at a commercial table, pushing for a people-led agenda that few others prioritise.

When your line manager, often the same commercial leader, controls your bonus and review, the pressure to stay quiet is intense. I've lost count of how many times colleagues voiced concerns privately, only to nod in silence when it mattered most. Often, the higher you climb, the quieter truth-telling becomes. If leaders at the top can't say what matters, psychological safety is already broken, and trust unravels from there.

Here's the harder truth: organisations may never create perfect conditions for courage. If you wait for safety, you'll wait forever. Voice doesn't follow safety; it forges it. Speaking up isn't about comfort; it's about alignment. Silence keeps the system tidy but stagnant. Voice shakes it, and that shake is what makes growth possible. Today, I'm strong enough to challenge when alignment feels false, to speak when silence feels safer and to know that if I don't, I'm complicit in my own disconnection. Integrity isn't about being liked; it's about staying aligned when disappearing would be easier.

Saying what matters will always feel risky, but staying silent costs more. Speaking up isn't about being right; it's about showing integrity. Over time, each honest word becomes a small repair in a system that's forgotten how to listen.

Politics and power will always shape what it feels safe to say. You can't control the room, but you can control whether you silence yourself. Voice is choice. It's sometimes costly, but always courageous. It's how presence builds trust in systems that need truth more than comfort. No organisation can hand you safety; you create it, one honest word at a time.

What it looks like when you stay silent	*What it looks like when you say what matters*
• Meetings full of nods but empty of truth. • You feel invisible even while available. • Misalignment festers because no one names it. • Decisions weaken because challenge never reaches the table. • You leave the room with a heavy chest, rehearsing what you wish you'd said.	• People know where you stand, and they trust you more for it. • Your voice becomes a source of clarity, not disruption. • Alignment becomes real, not just performed. • Teams grow stronger because honesty is normalised. • You leave meetings lighter, no longer carrying unspoken truths.

In your next meeting, name one thing cleanly and kindly. It could be as simple as, 'I see the upside, and I also worry about…' or 'I have a hesitation I'd like to surface so we can test it.' Notice not just how others respond, but how it feels in your body to voice it. That physical steadiness is the sign your courage is landing.

Over time, those moments of honesty ripple outwards. Teams start mirroring your openness, dialogue deepens, and the culture becomes less about agreement and more about alignment – a shift that begins with one steady voice willing to tell the truth.

PAUSE TO REFLECT

- What's one thing you swallowed this week that still sits heavily in your chest?
- What story did you tell yourself about why you couldn't say it?
- What would it look like to voice it next time, with clarity and care?
- Where could your honesty build more trust than your silence ever could?

Before we move on to the next anchor, notice how this research lives in conversation and what it looks like when a leader turns silence into truth and trust begins to grow in the space that honesty creates.

RESEARCH SPOTLIGHT:
Why Honest Voices Strengthen Trust

Most leaders hesitate before saying what truly matters. The fear is real: what if I'm labelled as difficult or my career suffers? But research increasingly suggests that silence often carries the greater cost.

Amy Edmondson (2019) has spent decades studying psychological safety – the shared belief that it's safe to take interpersonal risks at work. Her research shows that, over time, teams who acknowledge mistakes perform better because they learn faster, share ideas more openly and build trust that fuels innovation.

Deloitte's *Well-being at Work* study (2024) found that employees who feel 'heard, respected, and valued' are up to 4.6 times more likely to feel empowered to perform at their best. McKinsey's *Thriving Workplaces* report (Jeffery et al., 2025) likewise found that employees who report high levels of thriving – marked by purpose, psychological safety and social support – show productivity levels nearly three times higher than those with low thriving scores.

Yet not everyone experiences this equally. Women and underrepresented groups continue to report lower experiences of fairness and inclusion, not because they lack courage, but because bias continues to shape how candour and emotion are received (Nangia and Enderes, 2020). In these cases, silence isn't just personal; it's systemic.

> Neuroscience helps explain why truth-telling restores steadiness. As Daniel Goleman (2015) notes, naming what's real helps quieten the brain's threat response and re-engage the prefrontal cortex – the part linked to empathy, perspective and choice. Speaking honestly doesn't just clear the air; it calms the system and restores clarity.
>
> For leaders, the message is simple: when you voice what matters with clarity, you model courage in motion. Each honest word becomes a small act of repair in systems that too easily reward compliance over candour. Speaking up isn't resistance; it's responsibility – the quiet work of rebuilding trust, one conversation at a time.

Anchor Six: Let yourself be seen

In systems that reward polish over truth, visibility without vulnerability leaves you admired but alone. The final boundary is not about what you protect or what you say; it's about what you allow others to see.

For years, I thought leadership meant keeping the mask polished. Never showing doubt. Never admitting struggle. Always seeming in control. Behind that performance was fear – not of failure, but of being found out. Fuelled by old insecurities and the need to belong, I believed vulnerability was dangerous. At executive dinners, I often felt like a fish out of water. Leaders shared vacation stories, talking of ski trips and yacht cruises. I smiled, but inside I felt the gap. I hadn't grown up with those privileges. My school didn't even have sports facilities, and a near-drowning meant I had never learned to swim. The lifestyle they took for granted was a world away from mine. So, I compensated through performance, by providing fast answers, working long hours, delivering flawless results and trying anything to close the gap I felt but couldn't name.

Add to that the perfectionism baked into corporate life, the pressure to present flawlessly and the feedback about being a 'rough diamond' and my insecurities deepened. At one off-site, my voice shook during a presentation. The next day's feedback read: 'Brilliant content but lacks gravitas.' It stung. I spent months smoothing every edge.

Brené Brown (2018) reminds us that vulnerability isn't weakness but rather courage in motion. I read her work years later and wished I'd known about it sooner, because here's the paradox: the more polished I became, the less people trusted me. They connected with my performance, not with me.

I saw it in others, too. One finance executive I coached was known for her poise – impeccable slides, flawless delivery. Her team admired her but avoided approaching her. The turning point came when she admitted in a meeting, 'I don't have all the answers. I need your perspective.' She braced for judgement, but what she got was relief. That single sentence opened the door. Trust grew because she let herself be human.

When I returned to corporate life for eighteen months after my reinvention, the difference was profound. I no longer tried to erase my edges. In one high-stakes meeting, when I was asked a question I didn't know the answer to, I said, 'I don't have that data, but I can find out.' My throat tightened as I said it; the room went still. I waited for the old judgement, but the leader nodded instead, and I felt my shoulders drop. Relief. Then steadiness. It was a small moment, but it broke a lifelong reflex to over-perform. I wasn't as polished as others at the table, but I was grounded. I spoke less, but what I said landed. That strength didn't come from the system changing; it came from trusting that I am enough.

Corporate environments rarely reward vulnerability. They still prize polish, confidence and control. But if you wait for the system to make it safe to be seen, you'll wait forever. Authenticity isn't granted; it's modelled. Vulnerability isn't confession; it's connection – the willingness to be seen as human rather than perfect.

The mask may feel protective, but it quietly erodes trust. Letting yourself be seen is self-leadership in practice – the shift from being admired for performance to being trusted for presence.

What it looks like when you hide	*What it looks like when you're seen*
• You present yourself as flawless but feel lonely inside. • People admire your competence but don't really know you. • Trust stays thin because masks create distance. • Colleagues second-guess your reactions because they sense the disconnect. • You carry the pressure of always performing, with no space to simply be.	• You admit limits without shame, showing strength in honesty. • You give others permission to be human, too. • Trust deepens because people connect to you, not just your role. • Teams grow stronger because they feel safe to share openly. • You experience relief from the freedom of not carrying the mask alone.

In your next conversation, share one small truth you'd normally polish away: 'I don't have the full answer yet'; 'I'd like your perspective before I decide'; or, 'This part feels new for me too.'

Notice how the connection shifts when you show your humanity. Watch how others exhale when you do. Over time, this quiet honesty ripples outwards. Teams mirror your steadiness. Performance becomes partnership. The system learns to trust what's real because you trusted it first.

Here's the irony: when you stop performing, your influence expands, not because you're perfect, but because you're real.

PAUSE TO REFLECT

- Where are you still polishing the mask?
- What's one small truth you could share that would let others see the human beneath the role?
- How might letting yourself be seen build the trust you've been trying to earn through performance?
- What fear does the mask protect, and is it still serving you?

Before you turn the page, remember that in systems that glorify self-sacrifice, boundaries are how you stay kind without becoming depleted. Protect your energy so your yes carries weight. Say what matters so your voice builds trust. Let yourself be seen so people connect with the human behind the role.

Without boundaries, you become hollow – available everywhere but absent from yourself. With boundaries, you become steady, rooted, trustworthy and whole.

Like all anchors, this isn't about perfection. You won't always protect, speak or reveal in the moment. Sometimes you'll slip back into silence. Sometimes you'll say yes when you wish you hadn't. That's part of being human. The point isn't never to drift; it's knowing how to return to your limits, your truth and yourself. Boundaries are how courage learns its rhythm. They protect what matters, so authenticity can breathe.

7

Alignment: Leading From Within

In systems that reward performance over purpose, alignment keeps you from disappearing into success that no longer feels like you. Awareness helps you notice. Boundaries help you protect. Alignment helps you live what you know. Without it, old patterns return. You can be aware of the noise and protect your energy, but if your life is still built on compromises that clash with who you are, you'll drift again.

Alignment is what makes your leadership – and your life – feel coherent. It isn't about control or perfection. It's the relief of living as one integrated self – the steadiness that comes when your actions, values and presence line up. It turns resilience into direction and direction into peace.

This cluster of anchors offers three invitations:

1. Make space for possibility.
2. Let your values lead you.
3. Be all of you.

Each anchor helps you stop disappearing in success and start showing up whole and deliberate. They turn leadership from performance into participation – something lived, rather than proved.

Anchor Seven: Make space for possibility

In systems built on scarcity, creating space becomes an act of quiet leadership. Scarcity is the air corporate life breathes. There's never enough time. Never enough budget, recognition or seats at the table. Scarcity whispers, 'If you don't take this, someone else will'; 'If you say no, you'll lose your chance'; 'If you pause, you'll fall behind.' The system doesn't invent the fear; it amplifies it.

The structure often rewards speed and territory: protect your patch, hit the number, keep moving. The message is constant: prove, protect, perform or lose your place.

I lived this whisper for years. I said yes to projects I didn't want because I feared missing out. I stayed in roles longer than I should have because I worried nothing better would come along. I agreed to late-night flights even though my body screamed at me not to, because I thought credibility depended on always showing up. Scarcity kept me moving long after purpose had left the room. The harder I ran, the smaller my world became.

As Brené Brown (2010) observes, scarcity culture convinces us that recognising progress will dull ambition and that acknowledging good work risks slowing down drive. The opposite is true. Celebrating small wins restores energy and commitment.

Scarcity convinces us to keep running harder, even as the running erodes us. John, a regional vice president I worked with, lived this tension daily. 'If I stop moving, I'll lose everything I've built,' he told me. His calendar was a blur of back-to-back meetings. Strategy lived at the margins of the day, if at all. The politics of wearing two hats kept him cautious. In his functional role, he knew what was right for his people, but in his commercial role at the executive table, the pressure to deliver short-term results pulled him in another direction. That tension between purpose and performance often led to silence.

Through coaching, John began experimenting with space. He blocked out thinking time in his calendar, even when it felt impossible. He started voicing what others avoided: 'This timeline puts customer trust at risk.' He spoke more slowly but clearly. He chose based on values instead of fear, and the result surprised him. Instead of losing ground, he gained credibility. His team stopped mirroring his rush and started mirroring his calm. Meetings grew quieter and decisions sharper. The change began inside him, but the system around him softened in response.

Months later, John was still there – steadier, clearer and less reactive. The workload hadn't changed, but his relationship with it had. He'd learned how to stay in motion without being consumed by it. Sustainability wasn't a myth; it was a daily rhythm.

Progress rarely announces itself. It's built in quiet increments, in the unglamorous decisions no one applauds at first, such as the protected thinking hour, the slower meeting, the honest pause before a rushed yes. Repeated often, those small alignments compound until your leadership simply feels different – lighter, truer, more sustainable.

Possibility doesn't come from competing harder; it comes from having enough inner calm to hear what's true before the system decides for you. Scarcity narrows you; possibility expands you. That expansion begins not with abundance outside, but with permission inside. The system will always push for more: more meetings, more projects, more speed. Scarcity is baked into how corporate life is designed, but possibility comes if you claim space for it. No one else will block that time for you. Protecting space is how you model sustainability, for yourself and for those watching you lead. Space isn't absence; it's where clarity breathes.

What it looks like without space	*What it looks like with space*
• Every hour is filled, but the things that matter most stall at the edges. • You say yes to protect status or avoid loss, not because it serves direction. • 'No time' becomes both your story and your shield. • Urgency rules; strategy and creativity are always deferred. • You end the week exhausted but unsure what truly moved forward.	• White space exists in your calendar, and you defend it like you would a meeting with the CEO. • Ideas land because there's room for them to breathe. • You choose based on values rather than fear of missing out. • You feel more expansive, less reactive and better able to see options. • Others notice your steadiness and begin to follow your lead.

The next time scarcity whispers, 'Say yes,' pause to ask,' Am I choosing from fear or from alignment?' Even if you can't change the whole system, you can choose one response that is truer to you. That single conscious choice is where possibility enters.

Over time, those small choices ripple outwards, replacing speed with steadiness, compliance with courage and pressure with presence. That's how systems evolve, one grounded choice at a time.

PAUSE TO REFLECT

- Where are you saying yes out of fear of scarcity rather than from clarity of direction?
- What's one pocket of space you could protect this week?
- How might your leadership shift if you chose based on alignment instead of fear?
- What could unfold if you trusted that space creates results, not the other way around?
- What might open up if you believed that what's meant for you can only find you when you slow down enough to be found?

Anchor Eight: Let your values lead you

In systems that reward alignment with power over principle, your values become your compass. They are the quiet map that brings you back to yourself. Many leaders can recite their values, yet in high-stakes rooms, those values fall quiet.

I've done this, too, staying quiet in executive meetings where the agenda veered in directions that felt off. I told myself it was being pragmatic and that holding back was wiser. But the truth was simpler: I didn't want to be the lone voice speaking out. I didn't want to be labelled naïve or difficult. Silencing my values looked like professionalism but felt like disconnection. Every unspoken truth dimmed me a little more. Each compromise dulled clarity.

Susan, a senior leader in pharmaceuticals, reached that same threshold. On paper, she was thriving – promoted, respected, indispensable. Yet she came to coaching saying, 'I'm tired in a way sleep doesn't fix.' When we traced the fatigue, the pattern was clear: her values were constantly traded away in small doses. Integrity and inclusion mattered to her, but the system treated them as optional. Each quiet compromise cost her a piece of herself. By the time she found her way to coaching, her exhaustion wasn't about workload; it was about dissonance, the friction between what she valued and what she voiced.

Susan decided to stop waiting for the system to fix the gap. She began bringing her values into conversations, calmly and consistently. The first time she did so, her pulse quickened, and she glanced around the table, half-expecting eye rolls or polite dismissal. For a moment, the room went quiet. Then someone nodded, another added a thought, and the tension eased. 'How does this decision reflect what we say we stand for?' she would ask. It wasn't grandstanding; it was alignment in motion. Some meetings stayed quiet; others shifted. Over time, colleagues started coming to her for perspective, not permission. Her steadiness became its own form of influence. She hadn't changed her role, just her reference point. Her compass no longer pointed to approval; it pointed to truth.

Through twenty-five years in HR, working with executive teams in global organisations, I've learned that personal and organisational values don't have to align perfectly. That's not realistic. But if your core values – the ones you can't live without – are repeatedly compromised, erosion is inevitable.

Most organisations have values written on posters and recited at town halls, with words like 'respect', 'courage' and 'collaboration'. Yet in restructures, promotions or budget discussions, those values often blur under pressure. It's rarely hypocrisy; more often it's human fear of losing favour, status or control.

As Simon Sinek (2009) reminds us, people are drawn to why we do what we do – the belief beneath the work itself. When your actions reflect that belief, people don't just notice results; they trust who you are under pressure. Living your values out loud doesn't mean preaching. It means showing up in ways that match what matters most, trusting that coherence lasts longer than approval ever could. Values aren't slogans; they're signals. They show you when you're aligned or drifting, and expanding or eroding.

Organisations may print values on the wall, but they can't live them for you. Colleagues may stay silent, but only you know when your values are at stake.

Relief – and responsibility – come when you let your own values lead. That's the moment alignment becomes choice, and choice becomes leadership.

What it looks like when values are silent	*What it looks like when values lead*
• You nod along while unease churns inside. • You trade energy for approval, one quiet meeting at a time. • You leave the room knowing you've left yourself behind. • You start to feel fragmented, with one version of you at work and another everywhere else.	• You ground decisions in principles with simple, steady questions. • You feel energised because your presence matches your truth. • Others may not always agree, but they learn to trust your consistency. • You become known not just for results, but for integrity that holds firm under pressure. • Your steadiness invites others to return to theirs.

In your next meeting, bring one value into the room. Frame it as a question, such as 'How does this decision reflect our commitment to…?' Notice not just the answer, but how the conversation – and you – shift. Keep doing this, and you'll see the pattern: conversations slow, defensiveness eases, and decisions begin to honour more than deadlines. Over time, your one steady question becomes a quiet re-education of the culture itself. When your values speak, others remember theirs.

PAUSE TO REFLECT

- Which of your values is hardest to bring into the room?
- What do you fear might happen if you let it lead?
- What would shift if, even once this week, you allowed that value to guide your words or choices?
- How might your well-being change if you stop abandoning what you believe in?
- Where have you mistaken silence for diplomacy, and what truth is waiting underneath it?

Before we move on to the next anchor, notice how this research takes form in real life – what it looks like when a leader chooses to live their values out loud, and how that choice restores both trust and energy around them.

RESEARCH SPOTLIGHT:
Why Living Your Values Restores Trust and Energy

When leaders talk about values, it often sounds abstract – words on a wall or in a corporate handbook. But research shows that values alignment is among the strongest predictors of well-being, engagement and performance.

Simon Sinek (2009) popularised the idea that leaders who connect action with purpose inspire deeper trust and loyalty. His later work (2019) extends this view, suggesting that in a volatile world, those anchored in enduring values rather than short-term wins cultivate resilience that outlasts market shocks. Today's data confirms what many leaders already sense: values create steadiness when everything else shifts.

Gallup's *State of the Global Workplace* (2025) report shows that only 21% of employees worldwide feel engaged at work. Engagement and life satisfaction go hand in hand: half of engaged employees are thriving overall, compared with only a third of those who aren't. When engagement drops, daily stress rises, and one in two workers says they're watching out for or actively seeking a new job.

In essence, alignment between personal purpose and workplace values fuels energy, clarity and steadiness; disconnection drains them. For leaders, this isn't just a retention issue – it's a risk to trust, innovation and the health of the system itself (Gallup, 2025).

Neuroscience adds an extra layer. As T.J. Power explains in *The DOSE Effect* (2025), the brain's key 'feel-good' chemicals – dopamine, oxytocin, serotonin and endorphins – rise naturally when we live in ways that reflect connection, purpose, movement and rest. These are the same states that mark alignment with our deeper values. When we act against them, that balance falters, leaving us tense and drained. Our bodies register the gap between coherence and compromise long before our minds do.

Values-led leadership is felt, not performed. Leaders grounded in *why* speak with a steadiness that doesn't depend on external approval. Their decisions may not please everyone, but they ring true, and people sense the integrity behind them.

For leaders, the evidence is clear: values alignment isn't decoration; it's essential. It shapes engagement, retention, resilience and personal well-being. The invitation is simple but profound: know what matters most, live it consistently and let it guide your choices. The return shows up not only in outcomes but in energy, clarity and trust – the quiet foundations of sustainable leadership.

Anchor Nine: Be all of you

In systems that reward sameness, wholeness becomes your quiet leadership – both the hardest and the most liberating anchor.

For most of my career, I lived in fragments: the professional Rochelle who over-prepared and over-polished every sentence in meetings; the mother carrying the weight of raising twins and expectations that came with it; the friend who smiled through her exhaustion; and the private self who lay awake at night wondering if she was enough.

I thought compartmentalising was a strength. If I kept the pieces separate, then nothing would crack. But wholeness isn't control; it's integration. It's the courage to bring all the parts of you together and call them home. It's the quiet relief of no longer needing a mask for every room.

That pattern was amplified in corporate life. In global organisations, the expectation was always clear: sound polished, controlled, flawless. As a South African woman, English was my first language, but it wasn't the polished version of my British colleagues. My Afrikaans roots sometimes shaped my tone. I was direct, and my directness was critiqued for lacking gravitas. Instead of being supported to bring all of myself – the substance behind my words and the intent behind my edges – I was coached to polish. Each correction sanded away something real beneath. The sharper I became, the emptier it felt.

The first time I spoke in my natural way again – slower and less polished – my chest tightened. I waited for the usual wince or correction, but it didn't come. People nodded, as if they finally heard me rather than my performance. The relief was quiet, almost private, but it marked the start of something new. I realised I'd been trading belonging for acceptance, and they are not the same thing. Kristin Neff (2011) describes this as the practice of self-compassion: offering ourselves the same understanding and care we would extend to a good friend. For years, I gave that care to everyone else but never to myself.

The turning point came when I caught my inner critic mid-meeting and chose gentleness over judgement. In that small moment, integration began. I could be both direct and kind, professional and human, South African and global. Self-compassion turned what I once saw as difference into depth, and liability into strength.

I see this in clients, too. A male leader who hides his emotional side because he fears it won't be valued in executive meetings. A woman who tones down her warmth because she believes sharp edges win credibility. A manager who hides his health struggles because he thinks leadership means appearing strong. Each time they leave a piece of themselves behind, they fracture, and the rest of the room loses its fullness, too.

John, a senior leader in technology, shifted this pattern by letting more of himself into the room. Instead of only delivering sharp directives, he began opening meetings with a personal insight or a moment of pause. At first, colleagues were surprised, but over time, trust deepened. They didn't just see his competence; they saw him for who he was. That coherence made him a steadier leader, and it quietly invited others to show up whole.

Being all of you isn't oversharing. It's not spilling every private detail. It's allowing your edges to meet instead of performing perfection. It's when authenticity stops being performance and starts being presence.

Corporate cultures may reward polish or favour certain masks, but only you decide whether to keep fracturing or bring your whole self. The system doesn't grant integration; it's an inner permission – the daily act of returning to yourself. Wholeness isn't loud. It's a kind of quiet you can feel – the sound of having nothing left to prove.

What it looks like when you fragment yourself	*What it looks like when you're all of you*
• You switch masks depending on which room you're in. • You feel split between roles and never fully present in any of them. • Success feels hollow because it costs your authenticity. • You carry constant tension because you're always 'on guard'. • You perform connection instead of living it.	• You integrate personal and professional parts without apology. • You show up consistently, not performatively. • Trust deepens because people sense coherence. • Your steadiness shows; you're the same person in every room. • Your presence becomes quieter, but more magnetic.

In a work conversation this week, share something you would normally leave at the door – an interest, a perspective or a limit. See it not as exposure but as truth-telling. Notice how it shifts the connection. Over time, those small acts of honesty weave the fragments back together – in you and in the culture around you. Wholeness spreads through permission, not policy.

Every time you choose truth over polish, you make it safer for someone else to do the same.

PAUSE TO REFLECT

- Which part of yourself do you most often hide at work?
- What judgement are you most afraid of if you let it in?
- What would it look like to treat that part of you with compassion, instead of polishing it away?
- Where could integration replace effort this week?
- What would shift if you trusted that being real, not perfect, is what people remember most?

Before you turn the page, remember that in systems that prize performance over presence, alignment becomes the quiet evolution that makes leadership human again. Alignment isn't about perfection. It's not about neat choices or flawless careers. It's about coherence – the steadiness that comes when who you are on the inside matches how you show up outwardly.

When you make space for possibility, you stop letting fear of scarcity drive your choices. When you let your values lead, you stop trading your truth for approval. When you bring all of you, you stop leaving parts of yourself at the door.

Alignment won't erase the storms, but it will give you solid ground to stand on while they pass. That steadiness – the sense that you are the same person in every room – is what people trust most. In a world obsessed with performance, coherence becomes the new credibility.

Before you leave Part Three

In systems that prize constant motion, coming back to yourself is the most important pause of all.

You've just walked through nine ways to return when the world pulls you away:

- Notice the noise. Listen to your body. Take the pause.
- Protect your energy. Say what matters. Let yourself be seen.
- Make space for possibility. Let your values lead you. Be all of you.

These practices are simple, but not easy. They ask you to choose truth over performance, steadiness over speed and wholeness over approval. You won't get it right every time, and that's OK. You will drift – that's what it is to be human. The work is about remembering how to return. Now you have a rhythm to help you find your way back – something you can carry into meetings, conflicts and quiet moments alike. These practices aren't for perfection; they're for remembering.

I didn't practise all nine anchors at once. They formed slowly, with awareness first, then boundaries, then alignment – each layer teaching me steadiness over striving. That steadiness became freedom. And freedom, I learned, isn't escape; it's presence.

These anchors aren't theory. They're lived tools that I use with clients, colleagues and myself on the hardest days. They've held me through conflict and change, reminding me that leadership begins in the nervous system, not in the title. They develop through repetition, not rushing. Even the smallest practice begins to restore what the system forgets – your truth. The anchors are here, but only you can choose to use them. Each time you do, you relearn the quiet truth beneath it all that you were never broken, only buried beneath the noise.

Here's the paradox: as you start to live differently, doubt will grow louder. It isn't failure; it's your old self checking if the new self is safe. In Part Four, you'll meet those whispers of doubt with compassion, so they no longer pull you back into coping and instead become signs that growth is taking root. Doubt isn't regression; it's recalibration – your system adjusting to truth.

Wholeness isn't something to find; it's something to return to. It was always there, waiting for you.

PART FOUR

WHEN DOUBT SPEAKS, WHOLENESS REPLIES

Courage doesn't arrive when fear disappears; it grows when we move with it. Part Four explores that movement, looking at how doubt shows up not as failure, but as a signal you're stretching beyond what's familiar. Growth will always stir up unease. The question isn't how to silence it, but how to stay steady enough to listen.

By now, you've walked through three stages of this journey. In Part One, you traced the system and its pace. In Part Two, you named the beliefs that keep you coping. In Part Three, you began practising anchors that bring you back to yourself. As you've tried those anchors in real life, you may have heard whispers: 'Careful… Don't risk it. What if you lose everything?' That's doubt. Doubt doesn't mean you're failing or going backwards.

It's the mind's way of quietly asking, 'Am I safe to grow like this?' It doesn't show up to sabotage you, but to protect you in the only way it knows: by shrinking to keep you safe.

I felt it when I stepped back from the identity I had spent two decades perfecting. The questions came fast: *Who are you without the title? What if you fail or disappoint those who made sacrifices for you to get here?* For a long time, those whispers held me still, until I realised something vital: they weren't going away. My work wasn't to wait for silence; it was to move ahead with compassion for the part of me that was afraid. No one else could do that work for me. The system around me only made the whispers louder. Choosing to answer differently – to move even when my voice trembled – turned doubt from a dead end into a doorway.

Think of these next chapters as a dialogue between your doubt and your wholeness. You may recognise the patterns: freezing when it's time to speak, feeling invisible, fearing relapse and worrying you're too much or not enough. Different stories, the same root: doubt protecting what feels fragile. These aren't weaknesses; they're human reflexes – thresholds where your wholeness gets tested and, with care, deepened.

In the next three chapters, you'll meet familiar whispers that surface when you begin to change:

- Chapter 8: The Fear of Being Seen – the voice of vulnerability
- Chapter 9: The Fear of Letting Go – the voice of survival
- Chapter 10: The Fear of Becoming – the voice of transformation

Fear speaks through the body; doubt speaks through the mind. These chapters bring both into one conversation, because growth asks you to listen to each without letting either lead. As you read, notice what stings because it's usually closest to truth. Recognise doubt as protection, not proof. Experiment gently. Small steps are still steps, and with practice, you'll meet them differently. Doubt isn't regression; it's recalibration – your system testing how much safety you can hold while you grow. Often, it's smoke from an old story – pause, look and ask what's really burning. That's how you know you're growing.

Each of the chapters invites you to listen to a different voice of doubt and to practise answering from a place of steadiness rather than defence. You're not broken for feeling doubt; you're simply human. Keep the rhythm close: Notice → Anchor → Choose → Return.

8
The Fear Of Being Seen

The whisper of isolation that tells you everyone else is coping better than you. It's the fear that hides behind polish – the instinct to manage perception until nothing authentic shows. You feel it before you speak up in a meeting, share a half-formed idea or admit you're tired. That tightening is your body flagging social risk; the mind follows by forming doubt.

Fear of exposure rarely shouts; it refines you until you disappear. You look around the office, and everyone seems fine – calm, composed, on top of it. The leader who always has the right answer. The colleague who never seems fazed. The friend who posts family photos and holidays with a smile that says everything is perfect. Inside, you're exhausted – jaw tight, mind racing, sleep unsettled. Then comes the whisper, 'Maybe it's just me.'

It convinces you that everyone else is managing, so you stay silent and try to match them.

Appearances lie. Stillness can be shut down; silence can signify compliance; composure can be performance. Isolation rarely announces itself; it hides in disguise. For some leaders, it shows up as professional invisibility: they deliver solidly yet feel unseen. For others, it's the comparison trap – measuring your messiness inside against everyone else's polished outside. In meetings, it sounds like swallowed questions; in everyday talk, surface connection. Different costumes, the same whisper: 'You're alone.'

This isn't weakness; it's conditioning, shaped by early lessons that teach us safety lies in fitting in and appearing composed. We learn comparison early – who finishes first, who scores highest, who looks calm even when anxious inside. The irony? Almost everyone else is thinking the same thing.

One client, a rising leader, admitted that every Friday night, she sat in her car before going home and cried for ten minutes just to release the pressure. By Monday, she was composed again, and no one suspected a thing. She told herself, 'If I admit how much I'm struggling, they'll think I'm not cut out for leadership.' It wasn't true. Her performance reviews were excellent, but isolation convinced her she was failing alone.

I knew this whisper well. In leadership meetings, I'd look around at calm, certain faces while I rehearsed every word, heart pounding, telling myself, *'See? They're fine. You're the only one who feels this way.'* Later, in corridors and quiet chats, the truth surfaced. Those same colleagues admitted to exhaustion, doubt and a fear of being found out. That's the power of isolation. It's rarely the truth; it's rehearsal. The moment someone risks honesty, the illusion begins to loosen.

A senior leadership team I once coached embodied this pattern. On paper, they were exceptional – strategic, calm, aligned. Yet the corridors told a different story. In one-to-ones, leaders admitted to having doubts about a major project timeline. They worried about the risks of pushing ahead too fast and the impact on customers, but none of this was spoken aloud in the room, because they each believed they were the only ones questioning it.

When one leader finally raised the concern – naming the risk and linking it back to the customer – something shifted. Others leaned in. Questions surfaced. Instead of brushing it off, people began asking what was really behind the unease. One by one, voices joined in. Far from derailing progress, the honesty created it. Decisions became sharper because they were tested, not just nodded through.

In coaching, I saw it in David, a regional operations head, who often sensed when decisions were off-track but stayed quiet, fearing he'd seem difficult. When he finally said, 'I'm concerned about what this means for the customer experience,' others admitted the same doubts. What he thought would expose him built trust.

Another client, a senior woman in pharmaceuticals, said she felt invisible in virtual meetings: 'Everyone else looks so confident on camera. I freeze, praying no one asks my opinion.' When she began adding one honest line per call – 'This part feels unclear to me' – colleagues messaged their relief. Her honesty broke the spell of isolation.

In my corporate years, I saw the same. Peter, a capable mid-career professional, delivered flawlessly yet felt unseen. 'I sometimes feel like I could disappear and no one would notice,' he told me. His reviews were strong, but the whisper of isolation convinced him otherwise.

Three very different people in different contexts – David, the operations head; a global pharmaceuticals leader; and Peter, the steady professional who felt unseen – in different industries with different disguises, but the same whisper. Isolation isn't yours alone; it's a shared human pattern.

Honesty doesn't isolate us; it connects us. Brené Brown (2012) explains that shame feeds on secrecy, silence and self-judgement, but empathy starves it. When we believe we're alone in our struggle, shame keeps us quiet. The moment we risk honesty, connection becomes possible, and the illusion of isolation begins to loosen its hold.

Here's the part that matters most: no organisation can take this risk for you – structures built on performance and output reward composure, not vulnerability. If you wait for the room to make it safe, you may wait forever. The first crack in isolation is always yours to make. When you believe safety lies in being unseen, it shows up in familiar, repeated patterns.

Here's what that pattern often looks like in daily leadership.

When the fear of being seen drives you...	*It costs you in...*
Over-performance – working to prove worth rather than add value.	Self-visibility – people see output, not you.
Silence in meetings – holding back to look composed.	Influence – decisions move on without your signal.
Comparison – measuring what's inside against what others show outside.	Self-trust – confidence thins through constant self-editing.
Low-profile delivery – work lands, but your voice doesn't.	Credit – ideas are used without your name.

Whatever the form, the result is the same: you retreat inwardly, tightening the mask until the façade feels real. The harder you try to look fine, the more invisible your needs become. The mask that protects you also prevents others from reaching you.

The shift begins here with recognising that honesty isn't weakness but strength. You're not the only one, and what you feel isn't failure; it's humanity. Every honest word you share gives others permission to breathe. People don't trust perfection; they trust what's real.

This is how doubt begins to transform. When you meet the whisper with honesty, you shift from isolation to connection and from protection to presence. Fear wants you to hide; doubt asks if you'll risk being seen. The work of wholeness is learning to answer both with steady truth. The choice to voice even one truth rests with you. No system, team or culture will do it on your behalf. The invitation to step out of isolation is one only you can accept.

Next time you hear the whisper, 'Maybe it's just me?', pause and ask yourself, 'Am I comparing my inner experience to someone else's outer picture?' Then take one small step of honesty. It doesn't need to be big. It might be saying in a meeting, 'I have some doubts about this; can we explore those?' It might be telling a colleague, 'This pace feels unsustainable – how are you experiencing it?' It might be texting a friend, 'Honestly, today was hard.' Each small act chips away at the illusion of isolation.

PAUSE TO REFLECT

- Where do you most hear this whisper – in leadership meetings, at home, in friendships?
- Who do you compare yourself to most often?

- What would it feel like to tell even one person the truth, instead of carrying it alone?
- Who in your world might be quietly waiting for your honesty to open the door?

Doubt whispers: 'Don't speak. You're the only one.'

Wholeness replies: 'You're not alone. Your honesty is what makes connection possible.'

What follows in the research shows why honesty is never weakness; it's the beginning of real connection.

RESEARCH SPOTLIGHT:
Why Connection Strengthens Leadership

Isolation is one of the most common yet least spoken-about experiences in leadership. On the surface, leaders appear composed and connected. Underneath, many quietly admit to feeling alone in their struggles.

Brené Brown's (2012) research on shame and connection shows that silence fuels isolation. The belief that we are the only ones struggling convinces us to hide our difficulties, which, in turn, reinforces loneliness. The moment one person risks honesty, empathy becomes possible, and connection begins to form.

Deloitte's *Well-being at Work* survey (2024) notes that many leaders describe emotional exhaustion and disconnection as major barriers to sustainable performance. The study highlights that belonging and meaningful connection are essential foundations for long-term human sustainability. Gallup's (2025) *State of the Global Workplace* report echoes this: only 21% of employees worldwide feel engaged, 40% report daily stress, and one in five say they often feel lonely. Manager well-being has fallen sharply, particularly among women and older managers, with Gallup warning that disconnection at leadership levels threatens overall productivity.

Neuroscience helps explain why. Matthew Lieberman (2013) demonstrates that social exclusion activates many of the same neural pathways as physical pain. Feeling left out of a decision or unseen in a meeting doesn't just hurt emotionally; the brain registers it as a threat.

The hopeful insight is that connection can be rebuilt through small acts of honesty. Both Brown's (2012) and Edmondson's (2019) research on psychological safety shows that when leaders name uncertainty or share struggles, trust and collaboration deepen. Each moment of openness signals safety, and safety restores connection and strengthens collective resilience. The whisper, 'Am I the only one?' is answered not by perfection, but by presence.

Before you turn the page, pause and ask yourself, 'Where do I still hide behind composure?' Notice the rooms in which you shrink and the conversations where honesty feels risky. You don't need to expose everything at once, just begin where the whisper is loudest.

Each time you choose truth over polish and connection over performance, you rebuild trust in yourself. The fear of being seen softens not by disappearing, but by being met with presence.

9
The Fear Of Letting Go

The whisper that says, *'If I draw the line, I'll lose everything I've built.'* You feel it when the late-night ping arrives from your boss, when your calendar's already full but you say yes to another request anyway, and when you push through fatigue because slowing down feels unsafe.

This fear doesn't come from laziness; it comes from loyalty. It convinces you that worth and belonging depend on constantly proving yourself. You feel it the moment you even think about setting a boundary. The voice slips in, soft enough to sound like logic: *'What if this makes you look difficult? What if you say no and they stop trusting you? What if you stand your ground and they decide you're expendable?'*

Fear doesn't shout; it whispers. It makes overworking feel noble and limits feel dangerous. It tells you survival depends on silence, endless yeses, and pushing through no matter what. It convinces you that authenticity is too costly. Fear's job is protection, not truth. Doubt lives in the mind; fear starts in the body. The body senses risk first; then the ego – the over-protective inner manager – spins stories to keep things feeling familiar and safe.

I know this voice. For years, I equated availability with value. If my calendar was full, my inbox was cleared at midnight, and I never said no, surely I was proving my worth. But the truth was harder: the whisper of fear didn't keep me safe. It kept me performing while I slowly disappeared from my own life.

I learned this in the small, ordinary moments. Sunday nights in a quiet kitchen, batch-cooking for the week ahead while my laptop glowed on the counter with one more 'quick question'. A half-packed suitcase in the bedroom. School calendars on the notice board with colour-coded activities arranged around red-eye flights.

I was the lead earner in our family, yet married to someone with traditional views of marriage. I carried the weight of restructures, long-haul travel and hard decisions at work, while being the default parent and household project manager at home. If it needed to be planned, I planned it. If it needed to be absorbed, I absorbed it.

On the surface, I looked capable. Inside, I was frayed. Still, fear kept me moving, convincing me that endurance proved strength. I told myself this was what strength looked like, but strength isn't endurance; it's awareness.

The fear of loss doesn't always concern the big things, such as losing a job or missing a promotion. More often, it hides in smaller disguises: *'If I say no now, I'll disappear from their radar'*; *'If I protect my time, my income will be at risk'*; *'If I hold my line, they'll stop including me'*; or, *'If I push back, I'll be labelled difficult or uncooperative.'* Different masks, the same whisper: *'If you draw the line, you'll lose everything.'* It's learned conditioning – survival beliefs protecting belonging and control.

Ashley, a finance executive I coached, carried the same whisper. On paper, he was exceptional: a reliable deliverer with strong results and a reputation for being the one you could always call. But when he sat down in my office, he said quietly, 'I'm delivering, but I feel invisible.' He believed that constant yeses were the safest route to recognition. The more he absorbed, the more his presence faded.

We started with something small – one clear response under pressure. The first test came fast. The CFO pinged him late on a Wednesday: 'Need the analysis and slides by Friday morning.' Ashley took one breath and replied: 'I can deliver a full, accurate analysis by Tuesday, 10am. If you need something by Friday, I can share a summary view, but that would mean postponing the product-costing review scheduled for Thursday. Which option serves you best?'

After hitting send, he immediately felt sick. The whisper flared: *'You've overplayed your hand. They'll think you're difficult. You've just lost ground.'*

The reply came back within minutes: 'Tuesday, 10am works. Thanks for being clear about priorities.' No tension. No fallout. Just steadiness and quiet proof that clear limits invite respect, not distance. Over the next month, he tried it again in meetings, in project scoping and when dealing with ad-hoc requests that used to swallow his evenings. Each time he outlined his capacity and offered options, the room shifted. People listened. His yes carried more weight because people no longer assumed he was always available. His workload hadn't changed; his self-perception had. Fear loosened as he tested reality instead of obeying its story.

I saw the same fear play out with Maya, a marketing director. She felt she had to approve every campaign draft and slide deck personally. Saying no to late-night requests felt like negligence. But the more she absorbed, the more her influence thinned, and her team stopped bringing bold ideas. When she finally began saying, 'This is good enough to release,' the opposite of what she feared happened. Her credibility rose, her team grew, and her yes began to carry real weight. Letting go didn't mean lowering standards; it meant testing trust, first in the work, and then in herself.

I saw this in my corporate HR career, too. Priya, a respected leader, had built a reputation as the dependable one. If something needed fixing, her name was on the list. If a project required rescuing, she was the first call. That reliability earned her trust but also trapped her. Over coffee one day, she admitted, 'I'm terrified of saying no. If I ever push back, they'll stop seeing me as reliable.' The irony? Her reliability already made her trusted, but because she never set limits, her voice was missing when it mattered most.

I learned this lesson the hard way. For years, I judged myself for not coping better. I told myself endurance was strength and self-care was selfish, but the truth is compassion, not criticism, unhooks fear. Psychologist Kristin Neff (2011) describes self-compassion as treating ourselves with the same understanding and care we'd offer a friend. I had given that kindness everywhere except to myself. The day I started acknowledging, 'You're human. You're tired. You're allowed to have limits,' the whisper loosened its hold.

The signal wasn't to stop caring; it was to stop abandoning myself. That's when 'risk' started to look more like truth. Like a smoke alarm, fear's sound didn't disappear, but I learned to check whether it signalled a real fire or the heat of growth. The real work wasn't just setting boundaries; it was rebuilding self-trust.

Each time I honoured a limit, I proved to myself that my worth didn't hinge on over-delivering. The fear softened because I trusted my steadiness more than I needed approval.

When you equate constant doing with safety, this fear quietly drains you. When this pattern becomes a cycle, it looks something like this.

When the fear of loss runs you...	*It drains...*
You try to feel safe by over-delivering.	Energy – you run on depletion, not recovery.
You take on more to feel secure.	Clarity – priorities blur; focus fractures.
You avoid saying no to stay needed.	Credibility – weak limits make promises shaky.
You equate being available with being valued.	Capacity – there's no room left for the work that matters.

The irony? The more you overextend to avoid loss, the more you lose clarity, credibility and connection. Control feels like safety in the moment, yet over time, it erodes trust, especially self-trust.

Fear confuses approval with safety; self-trust separates them. When you honour a clear limit, your yes becomes steadier because your no is honest. That clarity strengthens connection and makes your presence trustworthy. Thriving begins not by doing more, but by choosing consciously.

Ashley's lesson was also mine. For years, I believed saying yes proved my worth, but reality-testing fear made me visible. Boundaries turned my voice from background noise into something others leaned in to hear. When I finally offered myself the compassion I gave others, I saw it clearly: the line I feared most was the one that gave me my life back. Fear tells us boundaries will cost us everything, but the greatest cost comes from never setting them. Because when you keep hollowing yourself out for approval, you don't just lose energy, you lose yourself.

No system or culture will draw these boundaries for you. If you wait for permission, you'll wait forever. The structures may reward over-giving, but your choice to protect energy and voice is what restores self-trust. That's the quiet act of accountability – choosing steadiness over approval.

PAUSE TO REFLECT

- Where do you most fear loss – at work, at home, in your relationships?
- Whose approval feels most tied to your availability, and how much is it costing you?
- What one boundary could you set this week that feels both kind and clear, and what might setting it give back to you?
- What story does your fear tell you about what you'll lose, and what evidence do you have that it's true?

Doubt whispers: 'If you draw the line, you'll lose everything.'

Wholeness replies: 'When you draw the line, you gain yourself, and that's what makes your yes matter.'

The research that follows reveals how clarity and self-trust don't distance us; they deepen trust for everyone involved.

RESEARCH SPOTLIGHT:
Why Clear Boundaries Strengthen Trust

One of the most persistent doubts leaders face is the fear that setting boundaries will cost them. Say no to a request, and you risk being seen as difficult. Push back on expectations, and you could lose influence, opportunity or even security. It's no surprise that so many leaders default to over-commitment. Beneath that fear isn't logic, it's biology. The nervous system reads uncertainty as a threat, even when nothing external is truly at risk.

Kristin Neff's (2011) research on self-compassion helps explain how self-trust softens that fear. Her work shows that people driven by achievement often equate worth with pleasing others and that saying no can feel like rejection, not only of the task but of themselves. Her studies show that self-compassionate individuals are less likely to fear disapproval and are better able to regulate emotion and choose wisely under pressure. When leaders practise self-kindness, fear loses its grip and limits begin to look like steadiness rather than risk.

Neuroscience backs this up. Stephen Porges' *Polyvagal Theory* (2011) demonstrates how our social nervous system links belonging with safety. Disappointing someone can feel like physical danger. Each time we honour a limit and the feared rejection doesn't happen, the body relearns that truth and connection can coexist.

Gallup's *State of the Global Workplace* report (2025) adds another dimension. The report identifies unclear expectations as one of the strongest predictors of daily stress: employees lacking clear priorities are 64% more likely to feel stressed and are far less engaged. Manager well-being and boundary clarity also cascade. When leaders model sustainable workloads and recovery, stress falls and team engagement rises. A steady leader steadies many.

The lesson isn't that fear disappears; it's that self-trust changes the signal. Each small act of honest limit-setting rewires the body's expectation of loss into evidence of safety. Fear may whisper, '*You'll lose everything*,' but experience teaches otherwise. Boundaries don't distance; they define. Clarity builds trust, and steadiness sustains it.

Before you turn the page, pause. Where are you still saying yes when your body's already saying no? Notice the places where fear still confuses approval with safety. Each time you choose clarity over compliance, you teach your body a new truth: boundaries don't cost belonging – they create it. Fear may still whisper, but steadiness replies.

10
The Fear Of Becoming

The whisper that says, *'Better the version of me I know than the self I don't.'* It shows up quietly – in the job you've outgrown but can't leave, the habits that keep you safe but small and the comfort of predictability that can be mistaken for stability. The fear of change isn't about failure; it's about uncertainty. It asks, 'Who will I be if I stop performing the version of me that once kept me safe?'

This whisper shows up in two directions. Looking back, it murmurs, 'You burned out once. Remember how bad it felt? You can't go through that again.' Looking forward, it warns, 'You've built your whole identity here. It's too late to shift. Why risk it now?' This is the voice of hesitation. It tells you your past is a lesson, and your future is already sealed. It whispers in a tone so plausible you almost believe it. But here's the truth: if you experienced burnout, it doesn't mean you're beyond repair. It means your system was speaking louder than your schedule could bear. It is never too late to realign. Wholeness isn't about erasing the past; it's about returning to what's true in the present. Fear roots in the body, doubt lives in the mind, and the ego stitches them together in defence. Knowing the difference changes how you meet this whisper.

Sometimes this fear doesn't sound dramatic; it hides in subtler disguises. It might be the fear of repeating mistakes: 'I've fallen before; I can't bear that again.' It might be the fear of wasted years: 'I've invested too much here to change now.' For others, it's the fear of irrelevance: 'I'm too old, too out of touch, too late to matter.' Often, it's the fear of lost trust: 'I broke it once; I'll never earn it back.' Different costumes, the same whisper, 'It's too late to begin again.'

I know this whisper well. As I shared earlier in my own story, burnout wasn't one dramatic collapse but a long misalignment after years of giving more than my body or boundaries could take. When I finally began to meet myself with compassion instead of criticism, everything started to change. My energy returned, clarity deepened, and steadiness replaced strain. My body had never turned against me; it had been asking for gentleness all along.

I returned to the plant-based way of eating I'd grown up with. The weight fell away, not because of a diet, but because I wasn't carrying the same load any more. When the story changed, so did my state of being, and behaviour followed naturally.

I've seen the same situation in others. Simone, the HR leader I mentioned earlier, had lived for years as the 'company sponge'. By the time we worked together, she was drained, convinced it was too late to reclaim herself. Her body was speaking loudly, experiencing one health issue after another. Her fear wasn't only about exhaustion; it was the fear of repeating the past, of crashing and failing again. When she began practising self-compassion, boundaries became possible. She started to see her value as more than what she could absorb. As her choices shifted, so did her health. Compassion softened the past; boundaries reshaped the future.

Then there is James, a divisional director I coached. He had been overlooked for promotion twice, and the whisper of hesitation told him the window had closed. In meetings, he began to hold back, assuming his voice no longer mattered. What haunted him wasn't just disappointment; it was the fear of irrelevance – that his best years were behind him. When he began sharing his views based on integrity rather than effort, something changed. His presence in the room grew. People leaned in. Within months, opportunities began to come his way again. What looked like an ending was simply the beginning of a truer chapter – one that started with him choosing to show up differently. Movement followed his inner steadiness, not certainty.

Karen, a project director, told me she felt 'locked into' the career she had built over twenty years. The whisper said, 'It's too late to retrain. You've invested too much to start again.' For years, she stayed – restless and disengaged – convincing herself she had no other options. This was the fear of wasted years, the belief that past investment meant a fixed future. When she eventually retrained in organisational development, a field that better matched her values, she discovered that none of those years had been wasted. Her project and change management skills transferred well. Her credibility grew. What she thought was an ending was a bridge. The whisper of hesitation had lied: it wasn't too late; it was exactly the time.

That's what the whisper of hesitation hides from us: the past isn't a prophecy, and the body isn't a threat. Both are teachers. The past shows us where we've drifted. The body shows us what we can't keep carrying. If we listen, both invite us back. Like a smoke alarm, the signal is there to be checked, not feared. It doesn't always mean danger; sometimes it's simply the warmth of growth. As Bessel van der Kolk (2021) explains, the same systems that can wound also hold the capacity to heal. What once protected us can be rewired to sustain us. The body remembers, and with attention, it restores.

When hesitation keeps you loyal to the familiar, it quietly limits who you can become. Here's how that hesitation often takes shape.

When hesitation keeps you the same...	*It limits you to...*
Avoiding past pain – you stop testing new ground.	Dragging the past – it steers instead of guides.
Clinging to old investments, afraid to waste years.	A smaller future – choices narrow to what you know.
Fearing irrelevance and withdrawing before anyone else can.	Stalled learning – skill and confidence stop compounding.
Over-apologising for lost trust instead of moving forwards.	A reduced self-story – control over possibility.

Every pause, every misstep, every scar is information, and when met with kindness, information becomes direction. The future isn't a verdict; it's an unfolding mosaic, shaped each time you return to yourself. Wholeness doesn't demand reinvention; it invites remembrance – a quiet reclaiming of what has always been yours.

Here's the invitation: the world may keep its pace, the system may not soften, and doubt will still murmur, but how to respond remains yours. Presence is still your leverage, and self-trust is your quiet power. Let yesterday inform you, but let today define you.

The whisper of hesitation can feel heavier than most because it draws on your own history. It knows your tender places, your regrets, your scars. That's why it feels so convincing. But reflection loosens its grip. Naming the stories you carry gives you space to choose differently.

PAUSE TO REFLECT

- Where are you most anchored by the past, or by fears of the future?
- What's one story you keep telling yourself that makes it feel too late?
- If you treated the past as data, not destiny, what new choice would open up today?
- What 'too-late' story did you inherit from your culture, family or industry, and how might you challenge it?
- If every skill and scar so far were training, not wasted time, what future might open up for you?

Doubt whispers: 'It's too late. You've already failed once. You can't risk it again.'

Wholeness replies: 'It's never too late to return to yourself and begin again from truth rather than fear.'

As the research ahead shows, renewal isn't a restart; it's the body and mind remembering how to move forward together.

RESEARCH SPOTLIGHT:
The Science and Energy of Renewal

The whisper, *'It's too late,'* can sound persuasive, but both science and lived experience tell a different story. Renewal isn't a single event or heroic act of reinvention; it's a natural rhythm of being human – a process that restarts each time we pay attention to what still wants to grow.

Psychologist Carol Dweck (2017) describes this through the lens of a growth mindset – the understanding that our capacity isn't fixed but develops through curiosity, effort and care. Across her studies, people who viewed setbacks as feedback rather than failure recovered faster and adapted more fully. Renewal begins not with a plan, but with a quiet shift in belief: 'Maybe I'm capable of more than I thought.'

Neuroscientist and psychiatrist Norman Doidge (2007, 2015) extends this idea through his research on neuroplasticity, showing how even adult brains can form new neural pathways when we practise new habits or patterns of thought. Each repetition strengthens the signal, allowing the brain – once believed to be static – to reorganise itself in response. Renewal, in this light, is not only emotional but biological: the brain rewires, and the body recalibrates.

At a subtler level, David R. Hawkins (2014) wrote of renewal as energy. Fear and control contract, while courage, trust and integrity expand. Though his model sits more in philosophy than in neuroscience, it reflects a similar truth: openness restores energy, and steadiness replaces strain.

Together, these perspectives – mindset, neuroscience and energy – remind us that transformation is not about becoming someone new. It's about remembering what's already within you and letting it breathe again. In essence, renewal is a return – a steady reclaiming of life's capacity to restore itself.

So, when hesitation whispers that it's too late, remember that renewal is not a phase of life; it is life continuing and waiting patiently for your return.

Before you turn the page, pause and notice where the whisper of 'too late' still lingers in you – in the roles you've outgrown or the hopes you've quietly set aside. Renewal doesn't ask for reinvention; it asks for honesty. Each time you meet the past with compassion instead of judgement, you reclaim energy once spent on regret. The future doesn't need a new you, only the steadier one that's been waiting underneath.

Before you leave Part Four

In this part of the book, we sat with three familiar whispers of doubt:

- The first asked what might happen if you were truly seen.
- The second warned of loss if you set a boundary.
- The third whispered that safety lives in staying the same.

Each whisper came dressed as logic, asking you to stay small, keep coping and hold back from change. Yet each carried the same hidden truth: doubt isn't failure; it's protection, the mind's story for a body that remembers fear. Your nervous system is simply recalling old scars and doing its best to keep you safe.

You've seen that honesty dissolves shame and isolation, boundaries deepen trust and compassion loosens fear. Stories like Karen's remind us that becoming isn't about starting over; it's about returning to what's true.

You may have also recognised quieter echoes of the same doubt. The fear of being too much or too visible. The fear of not being enough: the impostor whisper that says, 'Soon, they'll realise you don't belong here.' The fear of rejection or criticism – that one wrong step could cost your place. Even the fear that hope itself is dangerous, that wanting too much might break you.

Whatever the form, the root is the same: the wish to stay safe. Beneath every whisper is the ego doing its best to protect you from rejection, exposure or old pain. These voices never vanish; they simply change tone, circle back, then quieten again. Wholeness isn't about silencing them – it's about learning to listen differently, to check the alarm before assuming there is a fire.

I know this firsthand. Even now, as I write this book, the whispers still come: 'Will you have enough to support your children? What if stepping away from safety was reckless?'

Some months flow; others tighten. In that uncertainty, the whispers grow loud. Each time doubt resurfaces, you meet it with awareness. Sometimes you name it, sometimes you sit with it, sometimes you simply return to what you can control. Over time, this becomes the practice: awareness, compassion, alignment.

No structure can silence doubt completely. It's part of being human. But how you respond – not with defence, but with awareness and compassion – changes everything.

Doubt speaks: 'You're not ready. It's not safe. It's too late.'

Wholeness replies: 'You're not broken; you're renewing. Return to what's true and take the next kind step.'

As we turn to integration, remember that wholeness isn't one grand act of courage; it's a rhythm – a way of returning, again and again, to what matters most, even inside systems that are not built for stillness.

PART FIVE
THRIVING WITHIN THE SYSTEM

Thriving isn't about controlling the system; it's about changing how we meet it. Real change begins inside, in how we respond to pressure, pace and uncertainty. When doubt speaks again, as it will, thriving doesn't come from escaping the system but from meeting it from a steadier place within.

Everything you've walked through so far is designed to build the muscles for what comes next: awareness, courage and conscious choice. Now comes the practice – small, daily tools that help you live what you've learned. Wholeness isn't proven in big moments; it's tested in the ordinary ones.

By now, you've seen what coping costs, built anchors to steady yourself and named the whispers of doubt that try to keep you small. Part Five is where insight becomes embodiment – the bridge from knowing to living and from understanding to practice, bringing wholeness into the rhythm of your days.

When I returned to corporate life after burnout, I discovered that wholeness isn't tested on big stages. It shows up in the seconds between one choice and the next. One day, a meeting overran as usual. The old me would have stayed quiet and caught up late into the night. This time, I said, 'I'm conscious we're overrunning; could we adjust the agenda so everyone's voice is heard?' The tone shifted. People felt seen. I left feeling lighter.

That's the reality of thriving within: it's not one big decision, but a hundred quiet ones – moments where you notice what's happening and choose presence over performance. Part Five is about those small beginnings – the quieter steps that help you thrive inside the system you're part of. Very few of us can walk away completely. Most of us need the job, the salary, the structure. But that doesn't mean you must abandon yourself in the process.

Burnout taught me this the hard way. I once believed escape was the only way to heal. Returning to leadership showed me something deeper: after the inner work, you can coexist differently and be connected to the system without disconnecting from yourself. The corporate world may still demand speed, but thriving begins when you stop matching its pace and start leading with your own rhythm. That's what Part Five is about.

Here, you'll find three practices:

- See where you stand – holding up a mirror to how you're truly doing.
- Meet fear differently – noticing what it's asking of you before you react.
- Create your life as a canvas – aligning what you do with who you are, one choice at a time.

Each practice is simple, but together they form a rhythm: noticing, choosing, creating. As you move through them, notice how small shifts ripple outwards. Real change begins inside and expands from there. Keep the rhythm close: Notice → Anchor → Choose → Return.

Before we begin, it's worth pausing to see what the evidence says. The research is catching up with what many of us have already felt – that wholeness and authenticity aren't luxuries, they're what make performance sustainable. The spotlight ahead shows why.

RESEARCH SPOTLIGHT:
Why Wholeness and Authenticity Drive Real Results

For years, corporate culture treated well-being and performance as opposites, as if caring for people meant lowering ambition. Yet research keeps showing the reverse: when people feel seen, safe and supported, performance doesn't soften; it strengthens and lasts.

Gallup's *State of the Global Workplace* report (2025), reflecting data collected throughout 2024, found that only one in five employees worldwide feels engaged at work, and that disengagement costs the global economy an estimated $8.9 trillion each year in lost productivity. But here's the nuance: in teams led by managers who model clarity, fairness and care, engagement and profitability rise together. Humanity and high performance don't compete; they strengthen one another. Gallup's data also shows that when leaders are open about challenges and communicate transparently, their teams report up to five times higher levels of thriving and trust.

Deloitte's *Well-being at Work* survey (2024) echoes this pattern. It found that employees are 2.3 times more likely to feel engaged and 3.2 times more likely to stay when their leaders take visible responsibility for well-being through healthy boundaries, inclusion and open dialogue. The same study highlights that authenticity – meaning leaders whose words and actions are consistent – doubles employees' sense of trust and psychological safety. People commit when they feel safe to bring their whole selves, not just their output.

McKinsey's *Thriving Workplaces* report (Jeffery et al., 2025) adds another lens. Teams led by managers who demonstrate calm and authenticity under pressure show a 26% increase in collaboration and innovation, along with higher retention. McKinsey estimates that organisations investing in holistic employee health and authentic leadership could unlock up to $11.7 trillion in additional global economic value, with more than half of that coming from productivity and engagement gains. The evidence is consistent across industries – emotional steadiness isn't soft; it's strategic.

Together, these findings show that wholeness and authenticity are two sides of the same coin. Wholeness keeps leaders grounded; authenticity makes them trusted. When presence, values and behaviour align, energy is conserved, connection deepens, and performance becomes sustainable. Wholeness isn't idealism; it's intelligent design. Systems thrive when the people inside them do. And when leaders lead from truth rather than performance, they create workplaces where humanity and results rise together.

11
See Where You Stand

The mirror I mentioned earlier takes form here – not merely as an idea, but as a lived reflection. The first step to living whole is knowing where you are now. Most of us don't pause to check. We keep going – performing, delivering, meeting the next deadline – until one day we wake up and wonder, 'When did I drift so far from myself?'

That's why this chapter begins with a mirror. It is not designed to judge you or tell you who you are, but to help you see yourself clearly, where you already stand. This reflection is personal – it's about how you're showing up. As awareness deepens, the system around you often shifts quietly in response.

As I shared earlier, the warning signs were there for years. Only when I put pen to paper and answered the uncomfortable questions did I admit the truth: I wasn't thriving; I was surviving. Gentle, honest awareness is always the first step towards choice. That awareness is a gift – the doorway to real change.

In corporate life, we measure almost everything – performance, profit and engagement – but rarely pause to measure presence. Awareness itself is data. When you see where your energy, integrity and voice are strongest, you gain a clearer perspective not only on how you're leading, but also on how the system responds to you in turn.

Now that you've glimpsed what steadiness can look like, here's how to meet the mirror itself. Next, you'll find the Wholeness at Work Self-Assessment. It's a reflective tool, drawn from over three decades of cross-industry HR and leadership experience, including twenty years at executive level. Long before I formally trained as a coach, my work involved sitting alongside senior leaders, supporting them through transformation, conflict, ambition and exhaustion. Those conversations, combined with my own lived journey, revealed recurring patterns in what erodes us and what sustains us at work.

The Wholeness at Work Self-Assessment consists of forty short statements – ten for each of four dimensions – where you can rate how true each statement feels for you, on a scale from 'rarely' to 'almost always'. Each statement reflects the real struggles and strengths I've observed in people, leadership teams and coaching sessions across industries. Think of it as a compass as well as a mirror – a way to see where you're steady, where coping may be taking over, and where you might be quietly drifting.

Completing it only takes a few minutes. What matters most is how you approach it, not the numbers you circle. Before you begin, get specific – think of a real, typical week in your life, not the ideal one you wish were true. Notice your reactions to the statements; if a question stings, don't skim past it without answering. That sting is your smoke alarm doing its job. Go gently. If your chest tightens or your shoulders rise, pause, take a breath and come back when you're ready. When you finish, give yourself space before diving straight back into meetings or messages. This isn't about proving anything; it's about noticing where you are.

You may find value in revisiting this reflection after a few months – not to chase a different score, but to notice the difference in how you show up. Awareness becomes steadiness when it's practised, not measured. Each time you pause to check where you stand, you strengthen your ability to thrive from within the system, even before it changes.

Wholeness at Work Self-Assessment

The Wholeness at Work Self-Assessment isn't a performance review. It's a pause for honesty – a way to notice where you're steady, coping, or quietly drifting, without judgement.

It explores four dimensions of wholeness at work:

1. **Integrity** – the alignment between your values and actions
2. **Resilience** – how you repair and sustain energy under pressure
3. **Voice** – your freedom to speak truth and set boundaries
4. **Presence** – your ability to stay grounded and connected in the moment

For each statement, rate yourself: 1 = rarely true; 2 = sometimes true; 3 = often true or 4 = almost always true. Add up your score for each dimension, then add all four scores together for an overall total.

If you'd like a printable version of the Wholeness at Work Self-Assessment, you can download it at rochelletrow.com.

Integrity

1. My decisions reflect my personal values, even under pressure.
2. I feel able to live my truth at work without hiding parts of myself.
3. I notice when I'm compromising too much, and I correct course.
4. I rarely say yes when I mean no.
5. I feel proud, not torn, about how I succeed.
6. I would describe my leadership as guided by my values.
7. I don't feel I have to pretend to fit in.
8. People around me know what I stand for.
9. I make choices I can stand by, even if they are unpopular.
10. My sense of self is stronger than my need for approval.

Resilience

1. I build small breaks into my day.
2. I can switch off from work without guilt.
3. My body feels energised, not depleted, most of the week.
4. I take signals like fatigue, headaches, or irritability seriously.
5. I feel steady under pressure, not brittle.
6. I recover quickly from setbacks.
7. I don't wear exhaustion as proof of worth.
8. I get enough sleep to function well.
9. I notice when I'm drifting towards burnout.
10. I know how to repair, not just push through.

Voice

1. I feel safe speaking up in difficult rooms.
2. I say what I mean with honesty and respect.
3. My boundaries are clear to myself and others.
4. I rarely swallow my instincts just to fit in.
5. I can say no without guilt.
6. I don't confuse being 'nice' with being truthful.
7. I can share my true feelings without fear that they'll be used against me.
8. My colleagues know where I stand.
9. I don't need everyone to agree before I speak.
10. I feel confident my voice makes a difference.

Presence

1. I can pause before reacting under pressure.
2. My body feels grounded, not disconnected, in stressful moments.
3. I bring calm, not reactivity, into meetings.
4. I'm able to stay connected even when conversations get heated.
5. I notice and name what I feel in the moment.
6. My colleagues experience me as steady and present.
7. I don't confuse shutdown with composure.
8. I can sit with challenges without rushing to fix them.
9. I notice when I've drifted into autopilot.
10. I regularly return to myself through breath, pause, or reflection.

Add together your scores for all forty statements and check where your total falls:

- **120–160 = Thriving:** You're deeply grounded. Keep practising; your habit of coming back to yourself is strong.
- **80–119 = Coping:** You're holding it together, but at a cost. Notice where compromise shows up. Small shifts can change your rhythm.
- **40–79 = Surviving:** You're quietly drifting. Don't wait for collapse; this is the moment to return to yourself. The anchors in Part Two are your guide.

For a deeper look, total your score in each dimension to see where you're strongest and where you may be drifting most. As you reflect, notice what stung or felt uncomfortable, what brought relief, what repeated across different areas, and what surprised you. These signals show where alignment has slipped and where awareness is already beginning to return. Your scores aren't a verdict; they're a snapshot that is useful today and open to change.

Consider your scores through three lenses:

- **Pattern:** What repeats? (For example, strong integrity but weaker boundaries.)
- **Pressure:** Where do scores drop most under stress, and where do old coping habits reappear?

- **Priority:** Which single area, if strengthened over the next three months, would have the greatest ripple effect on the others?

PAUSE TO REFLECT

- Which dimension surprised you most?
- What difference do you notice between work and home?
- Which question still lingers, asking for attention?
- What truth is this mirror showing that you've avoided?

If your results show you're coping or surviving, remember you're not failing. You've adapted to systems that were never designed for your wholeness. This reflection isn't here to shame you; it's here to help you re-anchor. Awareness opens the door; practice helps you walk through it.

Your ninety-day compass

You don't need a five-point plan. You only need one focus you're willing to live with for a chosen period. The assessment is your snapshot; the compass is your movement. Journalling is one of the simplest ways to keep the two connected. A single line a day is enough space to track what you chose, notice what shifts and see how far you've come after ninety days.

Rather than tackling everything at once, circle one area that feels most alive, urgent or ignored. Then choose three small ways to carry it forward: *one micro-practice* (something you can do in five minutes or less each day), *one conversation* (with yourself or with someone else), and *one safeguard* (something that protects this commitment when life gets loud).

For example, if boundaries scored lowest, for your micro-practice, you might set an 'end-of-day stop' alarm at 6pm, close the laptop and write one line: *Where did I honour myself today?* For your conversation, you could then align with your manager or a friend on your top three priorities for the week. Finally, you might block out a thirty-minute buffer after your last meeting to wrap up the day – your safeguard.

Use your dimension scores as a guide to shape these experiments. If your range is **low (1–3)**, choose the smallest visible action – one pause, one boundary, one honest sentence. Awareness grows in micro-moments. If you're **mid-range (4–6)**, notice the context where you drift most and decide how you could meet it differently. If you scored **high (7–10)**, stabilise and share one practice with your team; leadership deepens through example, not intensity.

Keep your compass simple. Practise daily if you can, but lightly. The point is presence, not perfection. Your journal can hold you accountable – one sentence a day to mark what you tried, what worked and what you'll carry forward. The next chapters will build on this focus, showing how to meet fear and shape your canvas while you keep returning to yourself.

Before you turn the page, pause and take in what you've seen. This mirror wasn't built to judge you, but to help you see yourself with more honesty and care. Whatever your scores show – high, mid or low – they're simply reflections of where you're coming from, not verdicts on who you are. What matters now isn't perfection or planning; it's staying awake to what's real. The next step is learning to meet fear with that same presence, so that the steadiness you've built here can hold when life speeds up again.

12
Meet Fear Differently

The second step towards thriving within the system is learning to meet fear differently. Because fear never really goes away. It shows up in performance reviews, restructures, team conflicts and on quiet Sunday nights when the demands of the week ahead feel too heavy.

Before we go further, a small reminder. Earlier, we saw that doubt speaks through the mind and fear speaks through the body. They're different messengers, but they travel together. Doubt questions your readiness; fear protects your safety. Meeting fear differently begins with seeing that link – you can't quieten the mind if the body still feels unsafe.

As you read on, notice both the stories your mind tells and the signals your body sends. This chapter is about learning to meet them with the same awareness, gently, honestly, from the inside out. Fear isn't only personal; corporate systems amplify it through power dynamics, unspoken expectations and the pressure to always perform. But while the system may spark the alarm, the meaning you give that alarm is still yours to choose.

For years, I treated fear as evidence that I wasn't ready. If my chest tightened before a big meeting or I hesitated before saying no, I took it as proof. Fear told me stories, and I believed them. It wasn't until I reframed fear as a signal, not a story, that things began to shift. Let's return to the metaphor that helped me most: fear works like a smoke alarm. Sometimes the alarm means there's a real fire – a breach of your values, a genuine risk. Sometimes it's nothing but burnt toast – a small trigger, an old story, something uncomfortable but not dangerous.

The system may trigger fear, but how you interpret and meet it remains within your power. The problem isn't the alarm itself; it's forgetting to pause and check what's really burning. A smoke alarm doesn't tell you what to feel; it simply asks, 'Is there a fire?' When fear spikes, you can apply that logic.

First, *hear the alarm* and notice what happens in your body: the quickened heartbeat, the tight chest, the urgency in your voice. That's your nervous system saying, 'Pay *attention.*' Then *check for fire* by asking yourself what value is at stake, what the real risk is if you act or don't act and whether you'd stand by this choice tomorrow if it were public. Finally, *triage what you find.* If it's a real fire, stop or slow the decision, widen the conversation and act from alignment. If it's just a small amount of smoke, buy time and ask for space before responding. If it's only burnt toast, regulate first, then move forwards. The goal isn't to eliminate fear but to work with it, letting it inform your choices rather than run the show.

Fear shows up differently for each of us, yet the logic of the smoke alarm stays the same. To see how this works in daily life, imagine three common scenarios.

In the first, you're in a leadership meeting and feel the familiar rush of your heart racing, dry throat and the urge to stay silent. That's the alarm. When you check for fire, you realise truth and impact are at stake, but the real risk is only discomfort, not danger. This is small smoke. In the moment, you might say, 'Can I test an assumption? I might be missing something.' If that feels too much, try asking a single clarifying question instead of launching into a full counterargument. Afterwards, note what helped you speak up, even if briefly, so you can repeat it next time.

In the second scenario, you fall into the over-commitment trap – the automatic 'yes' followed by quiet resentment. The alarm is the heaviness in your gut as you hear yourself agreeing again. When you check for fire, you see that your energy and quality of work are at risk. For now, it's small smoke with the potential to grow into a real fire if this repeats. In the moment, you might say, 'I can deliver A by Friday, or B by Tuesday. Which matters more?' Replacing the default yes with two options that reflect your capacity helps you maintain integrity. A simple safeguard could be a twenty-four-hour pause before agreeing to anything new that will take more than two hours.

In the third scenario, you're asked to do something that feels misaligned. Your stomach knots, and the fear whispers that pushing back will damage your reputation. That's the alarm. When you check for fire, you see that integrity and people impact are both at stake – the potential harm is high. This is a real fire. In that moment, you could say, 'I'm concerned about the downstream risk to our customers or team. Could we explore a version that meets the deadline without compromising A, B and C?' If necessary, put your concern in writing, capturing both the risk and an alternative so that others can decide with eyes open. Afterwards, record your 'because line' – why it matters and what you're standing for.

These scenarios aren't about perfection; they're about practice. Each time you pause, name the alarm and choose one small shift, you build trust with yourself. But in the moment, fear doesn't live in your head – it starts in your body. Your body is the first messenger, the place where alignment or misalignment speaks before words do. That's why the next step matters.

Sometimes you can't think clearly until your body steadies first. Try this: exhale for longer than you inhale, four times. Drop your shoulders and place both feet flat on the ground. Name three facts you can verify right now. You're signalling to your nervous system: 'You're safe enough to choose.'

Once your body steadies, the next step is clarity. Before you act, write one sentence you can stand by on Monday morning: 'I am choosing A because B value matters more than C cost in this context.' If you can't finish that line cleanly, you don't yet have enough clarity or data.

One client, a senior operations leader, felt frozen whenever she had to challenge her line manager. The alarm in her body was loud: fast speech, flushed face and the whisper, 'Say nothing. Stay safe.' When we practised the smoke alarm tool, she began to separate signal from story. In one meeting, she noticed the alarm, paused and asked herself, 'Is this a fire or just smoke?' She realised the issue at hand wasn't about her competence – it was about the risk of a rushed decision that could harm customers. That was a fire worth naming. She spoke up calmly and clearly, and instead of pushback, she was thanked for catching something others had missed.

Fear will always whisper. Doubt will follow, trying to make sense of it. Systems won't pause to make space for your nervous system. That responsibility rests with you. The system will keep testing your steadiness, and your power lies in how consciously you meet those tests.

When you name fear as the body's alarm and doubt as the mind's echo, you create a small space between reaction and response. That's where steadiness begins. The more you practise, the more familiar it becomes. Slowly, you'll begin to trust that fear isn't a threat; it's information – an inner cue calling you back to alignment.

As you finish reading, take a moment for reflection.

PAUSE TO REFLECT

- Where does fear show up most often for you – in decisions, relationships or your body?
- How do you usually interpret that alarm: as proof you can't or as a signal to pause?
- What one step this week could you take to test the smoke alarm tool – hearing the alarm, checking for fire and choosing your response?

Doubt whispers: 'Fear means you're not ready.'

Wholeness replies: 'Fear means you're alive. What matters is how you choose to respond.'

Before we look at how this plays out in practice, the research offers its own reminder that fear isn't failure; it's feedback. The spotlight ahead shows what science reveals about turning fear into clarity.

RESEARCH SPOTLIGHT:
Turning Fear into Clarity

Fear often gets a bad reputation in leadership. We label it a weakness, deny it or try to push through it. Yet research shows that, like a smoke alarm, fear itself is not the threat – it's information. The challenge is learning to tell when the alarm signals a real fire and when it's simply oversensitive.

Clinician and author Deb Dana (2018), drawing on Stephen Porges' *Polyvagal Theory* (2011), explains that our nervous system constantly scans for cues of safety or danger. Her work shows how even subtle social signals, such as tone of voice, body language or a shift in facial expression, can trigger a threat response. In ancestral terms, this helped us survive predators. In modern workplaces, the same circuitry can misread tension or uncertainty as risk, treating an ambiguous email or a tense meeting like a physical threat. Leaders then rush, withdraw or over-control, not because the danger is real, but because the alarm has gone off.

Daniel Goleman (2015) adds a practical lens. His work on emotional intelligence and attention highlights how micro-pauses and mindful awareness can quieten the amygdala's hijack and re-engage the prefrontal cortex, the part of the brain that restores perspective. Even a single, conscious breath can begin to lower the body's alarm, creating space to choose rather than react.

Gallup's *State of the Global Workplace* report (2025), reflecting data collected throughout 2024, indicates that stress levels remain at record highs, especially among managers. Much of this stress stems not from real crises but from perceived pressure, including deadlines, ambiguity or the need to prove worth. When leaders treat every alert like a fire, teams absorb the panic. When they read fear as data – asking 'What is this alert trying to tell me?' – they model steadiness instead of reactivity.

Seen this way, fear becomes a messenger, not a verdict. Sometimes the alarm protects you, warning you not to cross a boundary that matters. Sometimes it's just an echo of an old story. The work of conscious leadership is not to silence fear but to understand its language and to separate signal from story and the body's alarm from the mind's doubt.

For leaders, that means replacing judgement with curiosity. Instead of saying, 'I shouldn't feel this,' ask, 'What might this fear be showing me?' When met with awareness, fear shifts from tension to information and acts as a reminder to pause, not a reason to retreat.

Before you turn the page, take one quiet breath. You've just learned to hear fear differently – not as proof you're failing, but as information to help you choose. The next time the alarm sounds, pause long enough to ask, 'Is this fire, smoke or just the heat of growth?'

You don't need to be fearless to lead with courage; you only need to be present enough to listen. Each moment you meet fear with awareness, you strengthen self-trust. That trust is what steadies you for what comes next – meeting the system itself without losing your centre.

13
Your Life As A Canvas

The final step to thriving within the system is remembering this: your life is not a checklist; it's a canvas.

For much of my career, I lived as though life was a constant list of boxes to tick, a constant chase for rightness. The right title. The right house. The right way to show up at work. The right schools for my children. Even the 'right' kind of holiday. Each tick gave me a quick hit of certainty, a momentary sense that I was achieving what mattered. But the truth is, I wasn't living; I was proving. Proving my worth, proving I belonged and proving I was enough. The more I proved, the further I drifted away from myself and closer to the noise of expectation. I thought ticking meant progress, but constant ticking meant following someone else's outline instead of painting my own picture. I wasn't choosing the colours that belonged to me. I was being pulled by pressure, approval and external definitions of success.

The shift came when I realised that wholeness was not going to arrive through another tick. It wasn't waiting for me in the next promotion, a bigger house or a more polished image. It began the moment I started asking, 'What colours belong to my truth, and how do I keep painting even when the system hands me its own palette?'

When I finally stopped chasing external markers and began painting my own, life didn't become neat, but it did become mine. Each choice I made, old story I rewrote and anchor I practised became another brush-stroke. As I write this book, I am still painting. My canvas hasn't stopped shifting. I am building a business that I care deeply about, and yet I don't have the anchor of a stable income. That's real. It means I may need to take on a corporate role again for a time, not because I've failed, but because this is what living necessitates. You start, you stop, you add some new colours and paint over others. To thrive within the system is to keep painting, even when the palette is imperfect. That's what makes the canvas come to life. The picture changes, and that doesn't mean you're doing it wrong. It means you're fully inhabiting your life. The truth is, the system will always offer you its colours – speed, certainty, control – but you get to decide which ones you reach for and which ones you leave to dry on the edge of the palette.

When I look at my canvas now, three movements stand out: evolving, aligning and living authentically. They are not rules but rhythms. Evolving means growing beyond the stories and identities that once kept me small. Aligning is about bringing my actions closer to my values, even when the system pulls me elsewhere. Living authentically is showing up as the same human, mask dropped and presence steady, in every room.

These movements shape how I live, lead and write. They remind me that the goal isn't perfection – it's truth. They only come alive through practice, the small brush-strokes of everyday life that slowly create a different picture. What follows are three ways to live them, not as techniques for perfection, but as simple experiments in evolving, aligning and living authentically.

The four-week canvas sprint

Seeing the picture is one thing; changing it takes small, visible strokes. One way to practise is the four-week canvas sprint – a short rhythm of noticing, softening, shifting and sealing new choices.

1. In week one, you *notice*. Each day, jot down one line, 'Where did I paint over myself?' and begin to see any patterns that repeat.
2. In week two, you *soften*. Choose one of those patterns, pause, breathe and name your value.

Say, 'Before we decide, this is what matters to me here.'

3. In week three, you *shift*. Add one visible brushstroke that reflects your value and tell someone what you're trying.
4. In week four, you *seal*. Keep the colours that feel true, paint over what doesn't and write one 'because line' for the habit you'll carry forward (see Chapter 12).

Each week isn't a performance review; it's an experiment. The goal isn't progress; it's presence. Stay curious about what each brushstroke reveals. Practice sticks when you give it a simple frame, and a weekly review helps you see whether your actions are aligning with your values. Set aside fifteen minutes at the end of the week and use four simple prompts:

- Where did I add colours that felt most like me?
- Where did I paint over myself or hide part of the picture?
- What brushstroke could I add next week to bring the picture closer to truth?
- What do I want to appreciate about the canvas I created this week?

Each week adds another layer, sometimes bold and sometimes subtle, but always part of the overall picture. This is alignment in practice: closing the gap between what you value and how you live. Alignment isn't about balance; it's about coherence – the quiet steadiness that emerges when your days begin to sound more like you.

Authenticity lives in the small, visible lines you're willing to draw. Some are boundaries, some are choices, and some are words you put out into the world. At the end of the day, write one line you'd be proud to see on your canvas a year from now, for example, 'Today I chose presence over pace with [a person or decision].'

Boundaries often live inside this line. They're the strokes that protect the picture. You might say, 'I can do A by Thursday or B by Friday – which is the priority?' or 'I'll pick this up in the morning and confirm by ten.' Sometimes it sounds like, 'Happy to explore this – what would you like me to deprioritise for now?' or 'I can't take this on right now without compromising C. Here's an alternative.' Each sentence is simple. Each keeps you whole.

Authenticity isn't about announcing your truth to the world in one speech. It's about the daily brushstrokes that match who you are inside with how you show up outside. Over time, those strokes form the quiet signature of your leadership, visible not in what you say but in the steadiness you bring.

Here are two small strokes from my own week. At work, living whole meant raising my hand in a meeting that was running over and suggesting we review the agenda so everyone could contribute without it spilling into the rest of the day. It wasn't dramatic, but it honoured both the group's and my own limits.

In my personal life, it has looked like something quieter. Co-parenting has triggered the old urge to defend from time to time. Now, I pause, breathe and remind myself that the reaction I'm meeting isn't always about me. When I choose not to mirror it back, the ripple stops with me. None of this is perfect. It's practice through noticing, choosing and returning. These are the brushstrokes of everyday wholeness, and every week offers a new corner of the canvas to explore.

When you lead others, painting a few brushstrokes in public can shift the palette for everyone. Begin meetings with a brief moment of breath and purpose, like wetting the canvas before starting to paint. End with one sentence of appreciation for a behaviour you want repeated, adding a deliberate highlight to the picture. That's how cultures shift: what you repeat becomes what you create.

Before you move on, choose one brushstroke you'll try tomorrow. Write it down somewhere visible. When you lead from presence instead of pressure, you invite others to pick up their own colours, too.

If your life were a canvas, what colours would you have been painting with lately – bright or muted, borrowed or your own? Where have you been following someone else's outline instead of sketching your own? What one brushstroke could you add this week that feels truly yours?

Doubt whispers: 'You don't get to choose. The canvas is already drawn for you.'

Wholeness replies: 'The canvas is yours. Every day is another chance to pick up the brush.'

Before you turn the page, pause for a moment. You've just explored what it means to live life as a canvas, trading proving for presence and perfection for truth. Look at the picture you're painting right now: the colours that still belong to others, and the shades that feel most like you. Each small choice to add, blend or repaint is an act of return, not to the system's version of success, but to your own. You don't need a masterpiece; you need movement. Tomorrow will offer another brushstroke.

Before you leave Part Five

You've now walked through the three practices that make wholeness real in ordinary life:

- See where you stand – holding up a mirror to how you're really doing.
- Meet fear differently – treating it as a signal, not a stop sign.

- Live as a canvas – shaping your days with values and authenticity.

Together, they form a rhythm of noticing, choosing and creating.

Here's what I know from lived experience: thriving within the system doesn't mean you never wobble; it means you remember how to return to yourself when you do. For years, I tried to sustain this rhythm alone, investing in my work, family and responsibilities while quietly neglecting my own renewal. When burnout came, I had nothing left to draw from. What changed everything was finally turning inwardly: reading widely, journalling honestly and asking trusted friends to hold up a mirror when I couldn't. That's how steadiness began to grow again, quietly, beneath the noise.

Thriving isn't the absence of pressure; it's the presence of practices that keep you connected when that pressure returns. Each time you notice, anchor or choose again, you strengthen your capacity to live within the system without losing yourself to it.

Conclusion: Return

When you first opened this book, I said that others probably see you as successful, steady, capable and driven. What they may not see is the cost of that. Now, having walked through the beliefs that helped you survive, the anchors that steadied you, the doubts that whispered back, and the daily practices of integration, you know that cost more clearly. You also know it doesn't have to define you.

Think back to where you began. Maybe you recognised yourself in the polished professional who seems in control but feels frayed inside. Maybe you heard your own beliefs: 'Don't show weakness. Say yes to everything. Push through no matter the cost.' Maybe you felt the quiet exhaustion that follows you home. Wherever you entered, you've now traced the journey of what coping costs, and what it means to return. You've begun to see what I had to learn the hard way: the system won't slow down for you, but you can change how you move within it. The moment you start to steady yourself, you're already shaping more than your own day; you're changing how others experience it.

Here is what that looks like in real time. The metrics are red, three leaders are talking past each other, and you feel a familiar tightness rise in your chest. First, you notice it: the breath shortening, the quick urge to fix it all alone. Next, you anchor: one deeper breath, feet on the floor, a hand steady on the table. Then, you choose – the truest words, not the fastest ones: 'Before we decide, here's what matters most and what we can let go.' The room exhales a fraction. The pressure hasn't vanished, the pace hasn't slowed, but you've changed how it moves through you.

When the meeting ends, you return by taking a brief walk and writing two lines in your notebook: 'What did I feel? What did I choose? What will I repeat?' This is not performance; it's presence in motion. The paradox remains, the world still accelerates, but steadiness is no longer abstract. It lives in your body before it shows up in your calendar. That's the discipline of this work: it's not controlling the storm, but refusing to abandon yourself in it.

That's really what this book is about. Not a flawless version of leadership or the eradication of doubt. The truth is simpler and harder. We will drift. We'll continue to feel the pull of fear, approval and exhaustion. We'll forget and then remember again. But now we know the way back, and how to notice the noise, listen to our bodies and steady ourselves before responding. We're learning how to protect our energy, say what matters and let ourselves be seen. We're learning to make space for possibility, to let our values lead us and to live fully.

Awareness without action changes nothing. Every return is a decision. The work begins again each time we choose how to meet the next moment. The very doubts that once made us shrink can now serve as signals that guide us home.

We also begin to see that returning to ourselves isn't only about steadiness; it's about belonging again. For years, we may have shaped ourselves to fit rooms that never truly saw us. We learned the language, played the roles and wore the armour. But real belonging asks something quieter of us: to bring our full selves without needing permission. Wholeness restores the sense that we can stand where we are, as we are, and still belong. And belonging comes with responsibility: when we stand whole, we steady the space for others, too.

This journey began with a paradox – the one every modern leader lives within. The system moves fast, yet the body moves at a human pace. We were taught to match the system's speed – to optimise, deliver and adapt – but not to pause. Thriving, we've learned, isn't about keeping up; it's about staying grounded as the pace rises around us. In a world shaped by constant innovation, artificial intelligence and polarised noise, this truth matters more than ever. The pace will keep rising; complexity will keep expanding. Our advantage isn't speed – it's steadiness.

The beliefs that once kept us safe – overachievement, control, composure – can quietly drain our aliveness. Our anchors return us to what steadies us: breath, boundaries, reflection and presence. These aren't abstract ideas. They're what allow us to lead from awareness rather than reactivity and to build strength from stillness.

What we've practised here is personal, but the patterns we feel in our nervous systems also show up at scale in culture. That's why the Research Spotlights appear throughout these pages, to hold a mirror between lived experience and organisational evidence. The research tells us what we already feel: when leaders are well, organisations work better. But knowledge doesn't change culture; practice does. Each of us becomes a proof point for the kind of world we want to build.

These truths are not theoretical. They have lived through me, through every system I once tried to master and every mask I wore to feel safe. Having grown up in South Africa during apartheid, in a family of humble means, the life that followed – executive roles in global multinationals and assignments across borders – would have been unthinkable to the girl who stood in queues with her mother, learning what systems can do to a body. I carry both truths: injustice in my beginnings and privilege in my ascent. Those experiences taught me how to perform for the system long before I learned how to be whole within it. Burnout made me stop, and listening to my body made me begin again. Simplicity replaced striving; nourishment replaced depletion. The same choice I had to make – to live what I knew – is the choice that now belongs to you.

I see it in ordinary rooms. An executive who once filled silence with certainty chooses to ask the real question. A team that traded speed for safety slows for one minute and makes a better call. A manager who feared visibility speaks early and calmly, changing the tone of a quarter. None of this is dramatic. All of it is decisive. Culture shifts in inches that are repeated. The ripple rarely announces itself. It travels through tone, through the meeting you leave feeling calmer than when you entered and the family dinner where you listen instead of reacting. One act of steadiness changes the next, and the next.

Since learning these lessons, I've seen them take root in the people I coach – leaders finding calm where there was once chaos, choosing presence over performance and discovering that one honest conversation can shift an entire relationship. The tools in this book began as my own experiments in recovery, and they continue to ripple out through every client I meet. It always begins quietly – one person, one body, one decision to return to steadiness – and then it multiplies. I've seen it move through families, teams and entire networks of influence. Choosing wholeness isn't merely self-care; it's also collective care. Each time we return, we model another way to live in systems that still reward depletion. That is how a movement begins – quietly, in ordinary rooms, until the ordinary changes shape.

The deeper legacy is a generation of leaders learning steadiness before burnout, organisations built on alignment rather than exhaustion, and success redefined to include the human beneath the role. When I began this journey, a quiet phrase guided me: *freedom to shine.* Over time, I realised it was never about brightness alone; it was about reflection. Every time we stand whole, we reflect possibility back to others. Choosing wholeness isn't selfish; it's an act of generosity. Our steadiness gives others permission to find theirs.

I'll leave you here, where practice begins. Most of us can't step away from our work, and nor should we need to. The real shift happens when we bring consciousness into the places that test it most. The system is evolving faster than ever – algorithms deciding, markets oscillating, attention thinning – but humans still create the tone. When we take responsibility for our own regulation, we restore the world's balance point.

Every mirror we hold up, every boundary we honour, every honest conversation we begin, is an act of redesign that ripples outwards in ways we may never see, but others will feel. Systems change when we do. This work doesn't stop with you. The steadiness you practise is felt by those who work beside you, live with you and love you. Each return strengthens more than one life.

Tomorrow morning won't be quieter because you finished a book. It will be quieter because you begin again. Before the first notification pings, take one breath you can feel. Name one value out loud. Choose one boundary you will honour even if the day pushes hard against it. When pressure rises, follow the rhythm you now know by heart: notice the signal, anchor in the body, choose from alignment and return with kindness. You won't always do it perfectly, and you're not meant to. This is circular work – a practice, not a performance. Some days, you'll drift far and yet still find your way back. Other days, you'll catch yourself early and smile at how quickly steadiness returns. Either way, you're building a different kind of strength – not the brittle kind that breaks under speed, but the flexible kind that bends and keeps its shape. Hold that shape long enough, and the rooms around you start to hold it too. That is leadership. That's legacy. Not the loudest voice, but the clearest centre.

Picture it: a morning commute, traffic crawling, inbox already full. The old urgency stirs, and you feel the reflex to race ahead, to prove, to fix. Then you pause and take one slow breath. You notice the rhythm beneath the noise, your heart steady and shoulders softening. The world around you hasn't changed, but you have. You remember that anchored doesn't mean still; it means centred. The light turns green, and you move, not with haste, but with clarity. The rhythm of return lives in that simple choice, hidden inside the ordinary moments that once rushed past unnoticed.

Now you know what steadiness feels like. The choice is simple: to return, again and again. That's where thriving begins: to lead without losing yourself.

If you'd like to continue this work in coaching, community or conversation, the next page will show you where to begin.

Carry It Forward

The ideas in this book are only the beginning. It is what you do with them in the meetings that test your presence, the choices that stretch your courage and the pauses that bring you back to yourself that changes everything. If you'd like to take this work further in your own life, team or organisation, there are various ways we can work together.

Learn and lead from wholeness with the following:

- Coaching – one-to-one work that helps you reconnect with steadiness, rebuild self-trust and lead from alignment.
- Team sessions and leadership retreats – practical spaces to translate these ideas into everyday behaviour, strengthen trust and restore energy to the system.

- Talks and dialogues – invite me to speak at your company, conference or community forum to explore how to thrive within the system without losing yourself. Each conversation brings this book's lessons to life through story, evidence and practice.

Read, reflect and stay connected using the following resources:

- *Awakening to Wholeness: A Life Unmasked* – my first book and the foundation of this journey: what it means to turn inwards before changing how you work.
- *Embrace Your Truth: A Journal for Personal Growth* – a reflective companion to help you listen before you lead.
- Articles and reflections – read the posts and blogs I publish on rochelletrow.com, thechangecanvas.ch and linkedin.com/in/executivecoachhr.

I know that the work of renewal can feel out of reach, and not everyone has access to coaching or corporate programmes. Because I believe these ideas belong to everyone, all of my published books are also available as free digital downloads on my website. If someone in your world might need this message, please share it with them. Wholeness should never be a privilege; it's a birthright.

Whether you start with a conversation, a book or a shared workshop, begin where you are. Each small act of awareness – whether a pause, boundary or honest dialogue – is how cultures change from the inside out.

Because wholeness isn't theory, it's leadership, lived.

References

Brown, B. (2010). *The gifts of imperfection: Let go of who you think you're supposed to be and embrace who you are.* Minnesota: Hazelden Publishing.

Brown, B. (2012). *Daring greatly: How the courage to be vulnerable transforms the way we live, love, parent, and lead.* New York: Gotham Books.

Brown, B. (2018). *Dare to lead: Brave work. Tough conversations. Whole hearts.* New York: Random House.

Brown, B. (2025). *Strong ground: The lessons of daring leadership, the tenacity of paradox, and the wisdom of the human spirit.* London: Ebury Publishing.

Dana, D. (2018). *The polyvagal theory in therapy: Engaging the rhythm of regulation.* New York: W.W. Norton & Company.

Deloitte (2024). *Well-being at work survey: The important role of leaders in advancing human sustainability.* Deloitte

Insights. Available at: www.deloitte.com/us/en/insights/topics/talent/workplace-well-being-research-2024.html (Accessed 24 November 2025).

Doidge, N. (2007). *The brain that changes itself: Stories of personal triumph from the frontiers of brain science.* New York: Viking.

Doidge, N. (2015). *The brain's way of healing: Remarkable discoveries and recoveries from the frontiers of neuroplasticity.* New York: Penguin Books.

Dweck, C.S. (2017). *Mindset: Changing the way you think to fulfil your potential (updated edition).* London: Robinson.

Edmondson, A. (2019). *The fearless organization: Creating psychological safety in the workplace for learning, innovation, and growth.* Hoboken, New Jersey: John Wiley & Sons.

Frankl, V.E. (2006). *Man's search for meaning.* Boston: Beacon Press.

Gallup (2025). *State of the global workplace.* Gallup, Inc. Available at: www.gallup.com/workplace/349484/state-of-the-global-workplace.aspx (Accessed 18 November 2025).

Goleman, D. (2015). *Focus: The hidden driver of excellence.* New York: Harper.

Hankir, A. and Zaman, R. (2013). Jung's archetype, 'The Wounded Healer', mental illness in the medical profession and the role of the health humanities in psychiatry. *BMJ Case Reports*, bcr2013009990. https://doi.org/10.1136/bcr-2013-009990.

Hawkins, D.R. (2014). *Letting go: The pathway of surrender.* Carlsbad, California: Hay House.

Huffington, A. (2014). *Thrive: The third metric to redefining success and creating a life of well-being, wisdom, and wonder.* New York: Harmony Books.

Jeffery, B., Weddle, B., Brassey, J. and Thaker, S. (2025). *Thriving workplaces: How employers can improve productivity and change lives.* McKinsey Health Institute. Available at: www.mckinsey.com/mhi/our-insights/thriving-workplaces-how-employers-can-improve-productivity-and-change-lives (Accessed 18 November 2025).

Jung, C.G. (1959 [2024]). *Civilization in transition (The collected works of C.G. Jung, Vol. 10).* Translated by R.F.C. Hull. Princeton University Press.

Keng, S.L., Smoski, M.J. and Robins, C.J. (2011). Effects of mindfulness on psychological health: A review of empirical studies. *Clinical Psychology Review*, 31(6), 1041–1056. https://doi.org/10.1016/j.cpr.2011.04.006.

Kross, E. (2021). *Chatter: The voice in our head, why it matters, and how to harness it.* New York: Crown.

Lieberman, M.D. (2013). *Social: Why our brains are wired to connect.* New York: Crown.

Maslach, C. and Leiter, M. (2022). *The burnout challenge: Managing people's relationships with their jobs.* Cambridge, Massachusetts: Harvard University Press.

Maté, G. (2012). *When the body says no: The cost of hidden stress.* Vintage Canada.

Nangia, N. and Enderes, K. (2020). *Mitigating bias in performance management: ACT now!* Deloitte Insights. Available at: www.deloitte.com/us/en/insights/topics/talent/mitigating-bias-in-performance-management.html (Accessed 18 November 2025).

Neff, K.D. (2011). *Self-compassion: The proven power of being kind to yourself.* New York: William Morrow.

Nolen-Hoeksema, S., Wisco, B.E. and Lyubomirsky, S. (2008). Rethinking rumination. *Perspectives on Psychological Science,* 3(5), 400–424. https://doi.org/10.1111/j.1745-6924.2008.00088.x.

Perry, B.D. and Winfrey, O. (2021). *What happened to you? Conversations on trauma, resilience, and healing.* New York: Flatiron Books.

Porges, S.W. (2011). *The polyvagal theory: Neurophysiological foundations of emotions, attachment, communication, and self-regulation.* New York: W.W. Norton & Company.

Power, T.J. (2025). *The DOSE effect: Optimize your brain and body by boosting your dopamine, oxytocin, serotonin, and endorphins.* London: HarperCollins.

Sinek, S. (2009). *Start with why: How great leaders inspire everyone to take action.* London: Penguin Books.

Sinek, S. (2019). *The infinite game.* London: Portfolio Penguin.

van der Kolk, B. (2021). *The body keeps the score: Brain, mind, and body in the healing of trauma.* New York: Penguin.

van der Zwan, J.E., de Vente, W., Huizink, A.C., Bögels, S.M. and de Bruin, E.I. (2015). Physical activity, mindfulness meditation, or heart rate variability biofeedback for stress reduction: A randomized controlled trial. *Applied Psychophysiology and Biofeedback,* 40(4), 257–268. https://doi.org/10.1007/s10484-015-9293-x.

Acknowledgements

This book came together the same way most good things do – through real conversations, honest feedback and people who cared enough to help me see what I couldn't always see myself.

To my clients, thank you for your trust, curiosity and courage. After reading my previous book, *Awakening to Wholeness,* many of you asked me the same question: 'How did you actually do it?' That question sparked this book. Each coaching session, reflection and moment of truth we shared helped turn experience into practice and story into structure. You gave the work its heart.

To the organisations and leaders I've had the privilege to work with, thank you for the lived experiences that lie quietly behind these pages. Every story has been rewritten with care to protect confidentiality while keeping the truth that those moments revealed.

When it was time to test the manuscript, I gathered a small early reviewers' circle, including a mix of coaches, authors and professionals within complex systems, along with readers who represent exactly who this book was written for: thoughtful, purpose-driven people trying to stay whole in fast-moving environments. Their feedback gave me confidence that this book was heading in the right direction.

My heartfelt thanks to April Ho-Nishimura, Christine D'Mello, Han-Peter Gai, Jenny Landgren, Karen Rivoire, Linda Vettrus-Nichols, Marina Cvetkovic, Namrata Adsul, Nicole Heimann, Rozanne Leyds, Rute Fernandes, Teresa Mazur and Ambassador Terry Earthwind Nichols. Each of you brought a different lens and challenge, and your compassion. Together, you helped refine the tone, strengthen the flow and ensure the message stayed hopeful and real.

To Nicole Heimann, thank you for writing the foreword with such clarity and care. Your words held the essence of this book in a way that felt true to the work and true to the journey behind it. I'm grateful for your steady presence over the years and for the honesty and humanity you have always brought into my life and leadership.

To Christine D'Mello, thank you for walking beside me over so many years. We first met in my Unilever days, and since then you've witnessed my leadership up close, in the real pressures of corporate life and in the shifts that followed. You've held my work, my questions and my growth with honesty and care, and your perspective has travelled with me from my first book to this one. I'm grateful for the steadiness of your support and the friendship that has grown around it.

Writing this book became its own practice, not of attempting to master every lesson, but of living the few that most asked to be tested again. My anchors steadied me when feedback felt uncomfortable. Awareness reminded me to pause before defending. Alignment became the quiet thread helping me stay true to my voice. In hindsight, the process echoed Jung's archetype of Chiron, the wounded healer, teaching me to meet my own wounds with compassion and turn pain into perspective. As Jung suggested, the parts of ourselves we've tended with honesty often become the very wisdom we offer others (Hankir and Zaman, 2013). In refining this book, I was also refining myself. In writing it, I was learning to offer what I've lived as a gift to those walking their own path.

As a South African who grew up in a tougher environment, I've learned to see directness and strong language as honesty, not harm. For years, I reached for words like 'rebellion', 'battle', 'push through', 'fix', or 'control' because they carried the rawness of what I'd lived. Through feedback, I learned to translate that energy without losing intent: rebellion became return, so that battle softened to navigate, push through found space in grounded, fix shifted towards notice, and control reframed as practice or intention. Each change kept the truth but widened the doorway for empathy. What sounded like realism to me might come across as harshness to readers from different worlds. The challenge wasn't to dilute truth but to translate it, and to keep integrity while ensuring it could be heard. Those shifts taught me that tone isn't about taming truth; it's about making space for it to be received.

In many ways, this process reminded me that the work is never finished. Each round of feedback, each re-read, asked me to apply what I was writing about: grounding before reacting, aligning before editing, softening without retreating. The more I wrote, the more I realised that wholeness isn't something you complete; it's something you return to – one paragraph, one decision, one tone at a time.

To the team at Rethink Press, thank you for your support and guidance in bringing this book into the world. Having self-published before, I appreciated the structure, clarity and calm steadiness you brought to the process. You helped raise the quality of this work while allowing it to stay true to its intent.

To my sons, thank you for standing quietly beside me through the hours of work, the rewrites and the early mornings. You've seen the highs and lows and still met me with patience and pride. Writing this book less than a year after my first would never have been possible without your encouragement and belief in me.

To my niece, Melanie Peck, thank you for walking beside me with humour, insight and care. You've become my little encyclopaedia and constant source of light. By pure serendipity, on the day I submitted this manuscript, we found ourselves talking about Chiron and the wounded healer, and I realised how deeply that archetype had been living in these pages all along. Thank you for being both my teacher and my mirror, and for reminding me that healing and creation often travel together.

To everyone who has walked some part of this journey – clients, reviewers, colleagues and family – thank you. While only a few names appear here, many hearts have shaped these pages. Your presence, feedback and trust gave this work its steadiness.

The Author

Rochelle Trow is a coach, author and HR executive with more than twenty-five years of international experience. She has shaped people strategy and led transformation in global organisations, including Unilever, GSK, Astellas, Takeda and Onsemi, earning a reputation for bringing clarity to complexity and keeping humanity at the centre of change.

Born in South Africa during apartheid, Rochelle grew up with a strong sense of fairness and a belief that leadership should serve people, not just systems. After nearly two decades in London and now based in Switzerland, she brings a global perspective and deep understanding of what it means to lead across cultures and contexts.

Her own experience of burnout and reinvention led her to found **The Change Canvas**, a leadership ecosystem dedicated to helping professionals thrive in high-pressure systems without losing themselves. Drawing on her lived experience and corporate background, Rochelle works with individuals, teams and organisations through coaching, facilitation, keynotes and leadership retreats. Coming from humble beginnings, she is passionate about accessibility and inclusion, sharing free tools, reflection guides, articles and digital copies of her books on rochelletrow.com and thechangecanvas.ch, making conscious leadership resources available to anyone seeking renewal and balance.

Today, Rochelle continues to work in corporate environments as a senior HR executive while running her own coaching and writing practice. This portfolio career reflects her belief that purpose and livelihood don't always need to come from the same source. Beyond her professional world, Rochelle is the mother of twin boys, Tako and Zviko, and shares their home with two British shorthair cats, Lena and Simba.

The message at the heart of this book is the same one that guides her life's work – that thriving doesn't require escape. Through her writing, coaching and leadership work, she helps people find steadiness and fulfilment where they are, supporting them in learning to move with the system without losing themselves.

🌐 rochelletrow.com

🌐 thechangecanvas.ch

www.ingramcontent.com/pod-product-compliance
Lightning Source LLC
LaVergne TN
LVHW030920080826
845145LV00013B/2979

* 9 7 8 1 7 8 1 3 3 9 7 3 2 *